John Chavis

To my ancestors and parents,
Elisabeth and Benjamin F. Chavis, Sr.;

to my sister,
June Chavis Davenport;

and to my husband,
Paul Anade Othow

JOHN CHAVIS

African American Patriot, Preacher, Teacher, and Mentor (1763–1838)

by HELEN CHAVIS OTHOW

FOREWORD BY
Minister Benjamin F. (Chavis) Muhammad

McFarland & Company, Inc., Publishers
Jefferson, North Carolina, and London

The author gratefully acknowledges those institutions who have granted permission for, or otherwise provided access to, certain material reprinted in this book. For John Chavis's *Letter Upon the Doctrine of the Extent of the Atonement of Christ*: the North Carolina Collection, Wilson Library, the University of North Carolina at Chapel Hill. For documents from the Cameron Family Papers, the Ernest Haywood Papers, the John Chavis Papers, and the Charles Phillips Papers, as well as the engraved portrait of Willie Mangum: the Southern Historical Collection, Wilson Library, the University of North Carolina at Chapel Hill. For documents from the Willie P. Mangum Collection, the Papers of Willie Person Mangum, and other archival documents: the North Carolina Department of Cultural Resources, Division of Archives and History, Raleigh. For archival documents from Virginia, and for photographs of Washington and Lee College: the Library of Virginia, Richmond. For documents of the Presbyterian Church: the Presbyterian Church (USA), Department of History and Records Management Services, Philadelphia; except "Excerpts from the Orange Presbytery": the Presbyterian Study Center, Montreat, North Carolina. For deeds of Wake County, North Carolina: the Wake County Register of Deeds. For deeds of Granville County, North Carolina: the Granville County Register of Deeds and the genealogical department of the Richard B. Thornton Library of Oxford, North Carolina. For the list of African American soldiers from Granville County who fought in World War II: the *Oxford Ledger*. For material from *Historical Register of Virginians in the Revolution*: the Dietz Press. For the engraving of Tusculum and the daguerreotype portrait of John Witherspoon: Princeton University. For portraits of Dr. G. C. Shaw and Mrs. Sarah Young: Vail-Ballou Press, Binghamton, N. Y. For maps of Hill Forest: Larry Jervis, School of Forestry, North Carolina State University, Raleigh. For photographs of John Chavis's descendants (Appendix C): the Chavis Archives, Oxford, North Carolina.

Library of Congress Cataloguing-in-Publication Data

Othow, Helen Chavis, 1932–
    John Chavis : African American patriot, preacher, teacher, and
mentor, 1763–1838 / by Helen Chavis Othow ; foreword by
Minister Benjamin F. (Chavis) Muhammad
        p.   cm.
    Includes bibliographical references and index.
    ISBN 0-7864-0818-9 (softcover : 50# alkaline paper) ∞
    1. Chavis, John, 1763–1838.   2. Presbyterian Church—United
States—Clergy—Biography.   3. Afro-American clergy—Biography.
I. Title.
    BX9225.C516O84   2001
    285'.1'092—dc21
    [B]   00-52525

British Library cataloguing data are available

On the cover: An unknown artist's illustration of John Chavis conducting classes for both white and black students. *(North Carolina Division of Archives and History, Raleigh.)*

Manufactured in the United States of America

McFarland & Company, Inc., Publishers
  Box 611, Jefferson, North Carolina 28640
    www.mcfarlandpub.com

Acknowledgments

Sincere appreciation is extended to all of the following for their guidance and support received during the past twelve years. To the North Carolina Library and Archives in Raleigh, particularly to Mr. Michael Hill, Researcher, Mr. George Stevenson, and Mr. Stephen E. Massengill in the Search Room for their kindness and scholarly assistance; the staff of the Wake County Register of Deeds Office; the staff of the Virginia Archives in Richmond, Virginia; the staff of the Research Library and Archives at the University of North Carolina at Chapel Hill; and the staff of Perkins Library and Archives as well as the Divinity School Library at Duke University. Special thanks are given to Mr. William Erwin of the Manuscripts Department of Perkins Library.

My sincere gratitude is also extended to the staff of the James R. Shepard Library of North Carolina Central University at Durham; the staff of the Firestone Library, the Seeley G. Mudd Archives, and Spear Theological Library at Princeton University; the staff of the National Archives of History in Washington, D.C.; and the staff of the New Jersey Archives in Trenton, New Jersey.

I am also truly grateful for the photographic services of Mr. Jerry Cotton at the University of North Carolina Archives and Mr. J. D. Hinton of Raleigh; for the kind assistance of my colleague Dr. Joan Fitch in the National Endowment for the Humanities Seminar for College Teachers, who accompanied me to Tusculum at Princeton University, where she photographed the house and other scenes on Dr. John Witherspoon's estate; and for the kindness of the caretakers of Tusculum, Mr. and Mrs. Victor Steiner.

Special appreciation is given to Mr. Willie Kelly of Saint Augustine's College, who designed our family tree; and to Phil and Jan Butin, pastors of the historic Nutbush Presbyterian Church in Townsville, North Carolina, and the Oxford Presbyterian Church in Oxford, North

Carolina. Rev. Phil Butin provided me the opportunity to examine their records of Nutbush Church dating to 1822.

Special acknowledgments are also extended to Ms. Ruby Creech, who compiled the family tree of Tom and Sindy Holt of Greensboro, North Carolina. This tree is an integral part of the Chavis family.

I am grateful for pictures donated by President Emeritus James A. Boyer and President Emeritus Prezell R. Robinson of St. Augustine's College. I am also grateful for pictures donated by Mrs. Benzina Chavis Harrell, granddaughter of Mr. Sam Chavis, the founder of the Columbia, South Carolina, branch of the family, which moved to Richmond, Virginia.

Invaluable help has come from various centers of research: the Historical Foundation of the Presbyterian and Reformed Churches, Inc., of Montreat, North Carolina, from which Mr. William B. Bynum sent numerous articles pertaining to John Chavis; the Presbyterian Historical Society in Philadelphia, Pennsylvania; and the helpful staff of the Genealogical Room at the Richard H. Thornton Library in Oxford, North Carolina. I will forever be grateful for the assistance given.

I am sincerely grateful for the assistance given to the gravesite search by Professor Larry Jervis, Head of the School of Forestry at North Carolina State University in Raleigh. My thanks are also due to Mr. and Mrs. Roy Cloniger of the School of Forestry, who served as our guides during the first visit to the Mangum Cemetery as well as to other cemeteries in the area in 1987, and to Mr. Bret Wallingford and Mr. Mike Petruncio, who served as our guides in 1988. It was Mr. Wallingford who discovered the first stone to come into view in the newly discovered cemetery on the Mangum plantation—a cemetery that may enshrine the remains of John Chavis.

I am especially grateful to my fellow members of the John Chavis Historical Society who have actively participated in our search for the gravesite: Mrs. Vivian Chavis Ross; Mr. Matthew Wesley Chavis, IV; the Rev. Dr. Benjamin F. Chavis, Jr.; Mrs. Madelyn Pine, Ms. Octavia Chavis, and Mr. Franklin Pierce Ridley, Jr.

I would also like to express my sincere gratitude to my relatives who gave me moral and spiritual support while I took time away from them to engage in my research and writing: my mother, Mrs. Elisabeth Ridley Chavis; my sisters, Dr. LaRhoda Francine Chavis and Mrs. June Chavis Davenport; my brother, Rev. Dr. Benjamin F. Chavis, Jr.; my husband, Mr. Paul Anade Othow, and my daughter, Ajulonyodier Elisabeth Othow. Mr. Jordan Chavis of Nashville,

Tennessee, provided interesting details about his father, who was a descendant of Chavis.

Last and most importantly, I wish to express my profound appreciation to the United Negro College Fund for granting me a Distinguished Faculty Fellowship to conduct research on John Chavis; to the administration of Saint Augustine's College; and to Dr. Prezell R. Robinson, president, and Dr. Thelma Roundtree, vice president for Academic Affairs, for nominating me to be a recipient of the award in 1987. My appreciation is also extended to the National Endowment for the Humanities for awarding me a grant to participate in further studies about my subject during the summer of 1988 at Princeton University.

I am also indebted and grateful to Ms. Betty Holman, who tirelessly assisted with keyboarding various revisions of my manuscript; to Ms. Rhonda Towns and Ms. Drusilla Dunn for keyboarding the final manuscript; and to Mr. Don Donaldson for technical assistance.

All of the resources and persons mentioned above, as well as many not mentioned because of limited space, have contributed greatly not only to an understanding of the life and contributions of John Chavis, but to an understanding of American history in general and African American history in particular.

Table of Contents

Foreword

Helen Chavis Othow has joined the ranks of those authors who dare to venture back into history to discover facts that bear witness to eternal truths.

The life and legacy of John Chavis (1763–1838) are meticulously documented by Dr. Othow in a manner that illuminates aspects of the historical struggle and triumph of African Americans. The eighteenth and nineteenth centuries are blood-soaked with the history of slavery and all of its atrocities. Yet Dr. Othow goes a step beyond describing what is generally known about this period of history. Each chapter of this book reveals what is not commonly known: the fact that not all Africans in America were slaves.

Many Africans fought in the Revolutionary War, not because they were forced to fight, but because they sought to defend the land that they owned to ensure wealth and endowment for generations to come. In other words, the fact that a black man, Crispus Attucks, was the first American to be killed in the Revolutionary War should not be viewed as a surprise or a fluke; Attucks's service was not an isolated phenomenon.

John Chavis was a revolutionary soldier because his father and grandfathers were some of the largest black landowners in America prior to the Revolutionary War. In telling his story, Dr. Othow brings light and exposure to certain roots of the United States of America that are not commonly revealed or studied in traditional books on American history.

John Chavis was one of the earliest progenitors of the spiritual genius and intellectual prowess that gave rise to the irrepressible determination of African Americans to contribute to the evolution of the United States of America. Chavis became the first black ordained preacher-theologian of the Presbyterian Church. At the same time, John Chavis was a skillful freedom fighter who chose as his weapons the pen and the textbook, rather than the machete and other weapons used in slave insurrections.

Notwithstanding the risk of offending those who cling to popular and institutionalized stereotypes in regard to blacks, whites, and Indians during the first century of United States history, Dr. Othow uncovers a free black man's hidden legacy. Thus, the publication of this book refocuses long overdue attention on this period of history.

Adding to the value and quality of this work is the detailed genealogical evidence presented by Othow. John Chavis was born in 1763 in what is still known as Granville County, North Carolina. Chavis was part of a family whose roots run very deep in American social, economic, theological and cultural history. The fact that the Chavis family 250 years later still lives in Granville County further verifies the convergence of the family's oral history with genealogical and social artifacts revealed by Dr. Othow.

We certainly get more than just a glimpse of the growth and expansion of American Protestantism as Dr. Othow traces the sequence of actions of the Presbyterian Church in the South and particularly in Virginia and North Carolina. Dr. Othow puts the reader inside the deliberations of the Presbytery in the aftermath of the Declaration of Independence of 1776 and the Continental Congress of the United States in 1788. It is noteworthy how the church did not vigorously challenge the state legislatures of Virginia and the Carolinas on the question of repressive legislation occurring after the Nat Turner insurrection—legislation that prohibited blacks from teaching or preaching. Of course all of this is before the beginning of the Civil War, but thanks to the contributions of Dr. Othow's scholarship we are reminded of the intricacies of what could be described as pre–Civil War apartheid in America.

Another mark of distinction in this book is its transcendent presentation of John Chavis's theology of atonement. How is it possible for a free black man whose ancestors were African slaves to find faith in theological principles relating to forgiveness and reconciliation through Jesus Christ? John Chavis answers this question forcefully through his letter and other writings on atonement that he dared to publish in 1837 over the objection of the church. It must be stated that Dr. Helen Othow posits the love that John Chavis had for the Presbyterian Church as well as the entire Christian community. But his love for Jesus Christ was his greatest love, and he resisted ultimately the restrictions placed on him both by the church and the state.

As a descendant of the Reverend John Chavis, I believe it is more providential than historically coincidental that nearly 165 years after John Chavis's publication on the atonement, the Million Man March was convened by the Honorable Minister Louis Farrakhan in Washington, D.C., under the theme of atonement. I served as the national director of the Million Man March, and I know that God was truly at work in getting 2 million black men to come to grips with the theological imperatives of atonement. The Christian-Muslim unity displayed at the Million Man March shook the grave of John Chavis and of all the ancestors who have yearned and cried out for unity, freedom, justice and equality.

Through persistence and determination, Dr. Helen has completed this book on John Chavis. Through her generosity, she now offers it as a gift to the world in hopes that all of humanity will eventually atone and be free. We should all be very grateful.

Minister Benjamin F. (Chavis) Muhammad
New York, New York
December 2000

Preface

Many articles in newspapers and journals have appeared on the life of John Chavis, but very few book length studies have been reported (Shaw, 1931; Boyd, 1947; and Toole, 1956). This study brings together various sources to update the historical records. Through the years some facts as well as some myths have been reported. This book aims to reveal newly found historical documents, reports and first-hand observations which shed more light upon Chavis's ancestors, accomplishments, philosophy, possible descendants, and contributions to American life.

The book includes primary documents, photographs, and illustrations which authenticate the research endeavor. Some of the questions that are raised in the John Chavis scholarship concern Chavis's family background and early life; his education prior to going to Princeton University; his participation in the Revolutionary War; his matriculation at Princeton University and at Washington College in Virginia (now Washington and Lee University); his descendants; his life during his declining years; and his final resting place. The answers to most of these questions have been limned in these pages.

Since John Chavis, according to Charles Lee Smith, had the best classical secondary school "to be found in the state" of North Carolina in his time, it is important that updated coverage of his life and contributions be published (Smith, "History of Education in North Carolina" 1888). Thus we shall see that the patriot John Chavis, who fought in the American Revolution, respected those noble ideas which the founding fathers esteemed.

Janus-like, this study looks both backward and forward, tracing the legacy of John Chavis in the past and present. It is intended as a contribution to John Chavis scholarship, which was first begun at the University of North Carolina by Professor Charles Lee Phillips in 1883 and has continued with succeeding generations of scholars and laymen.

Part I

John Chavis: His Life and Legacies

CHAPTER 1

Early Life and Family Ties

Much mystery has surrounded the life of John Chavis, who according to historical documents was born in 1763 and was reported to have died in 1838. Even though he is known nationally for his preaching to all races and his teaching of white and free black students before the Civil War, there are conflicting opinions about his place of birth and family connections. In my family, the tradition that we are descendants of John Chavis has been passed down from generation to generation. My father and many of our elders have informed us at an early age about this revered connection. Therefore, as I have read the various historical accounts of his purported place of birth and the mysteries surrounding his family ties, I have been greatly motivated to delve as deeply as possible into discovering the truth. In the study of the life and contributions of John Chavis, I have tried to trace his footsteps from his forebears and his early childhood, through his youth, maturity, and age, to his place of burial.

When news began to spread in the 1880s about the remarkable achievements of Rev. John Chavis, a black man who had preached to all races and taught a classical school before the Civil War, many writers tried to explain what appeared to be a great anomaly for the time. Even after the Emancipation Proclamation, blacks were still held in an inferior status and had been disenfranchised of certain rights such as voting which the free blacks had been given the right to exercise from the end of the Revolutionary War in 1776 until 1835.

The interest in the enigma of Chavis's life is shown in the many written inquiries from the 1880s. A newspaper article originally printed in the *Raleigh Sentinel* and reprinted in the *Oxford Torchlight*, September 21, 1880, on "John Chavers" purports to be an interview by an unknown writer with a person named "Christopher." Christopher was asked if he knew John Chavers (sic), "a Negro schoolmaster, who taught Judge Mangum and Honorable Abraham Rencher."

Christopher answered, "I went to school to him myself." When asked what year he attended the school, he said either 1814 or 1815. Christopher also was asked if Chavis taught Negro children. He replied, "That you know was against the law."[1] However, free black children were being taught by Chavis in 1814 and 1815. He was forbidden to teach after 1831 (see Chapter 4). Christopher goes on to say that Chavis boarded with the pastor of his church and sat at his table. Of great concern among those who wrote about the venerable minister and teacher was the social equality that John Chavis shared with the leading whites. According to Christopher, Chavis asked the blessing at the pastor's table and preached to white congregations.

Another issue in the myriad questions about Chavis is his complexion. The great degree of speculation reveals the acuteness of the color problem in America. The interviewer asked Christopher about Chavis's color and appearance:

> "Was he mulatto or black?"
> "Black, he was black as coal."
> "What of his person?"
> "He was stout, not remarkable for height or want of it.
> Neat in dress, which was always of black cloth, and of the
> style and fashion of his day."[2]

When asked what boys went to school with him, Christopher replied:

> W. H. Haywood, the Senator, and his cousin, Stephen
> Haywood, Bishop Polk and his brother Lucien, Dr. Wm.
> Shaw and his brother, and the children of the best men of
> the town, for no man looked with contempt upon the
> preacher and teacher.[3]

Of course, there were many more children from the most prominent families of North Carolina whom Rev. Chavis taught. They will be mentioned in Chapters 4 and 5.

The interview ends with the questions about how Chavis died and where he was buried. Christopher said,

> I don't know where he came from or what became of
> him. He went from here to Chatham and continued to
> preach and teach, and never forfeited his good character.
> He had the friendship and confidence of such men as Dr.
> McPheeters, and maintained it to the last.[4]

History appears to contradict this last remark, for Dr. McPheeters was one of the members of the Orange Presbytery who read Chavis's sermon *The Atonement*. Chavis wanted to have the sermon published for subsistence, but McPheeters refused to have the sermon published under the auspices of the church.

As mentioned earlier, the interview contains some of the stock questions which have been speculated upon by subsequent writers. (1) Did he teach white and black children? (2) Was he an excellent teacher and preacher? (3) Did he preach for whites and blacks? (4) Did he have social equality with the white aristocrats of North Carolina? (5) What was his complexion? (6) How did he die and where was he buried?

We may note the historical period in which the speculation occurred. It was during the post–Reconstruction era, when there was a concerted effort by some factions to destroy the rights that blacks had gained during Reconstruction. This was the period of grandfather clauses and disenfranchisement. Even the right to a true knowledge of black history could be tampered with.

There were two factions in North Carolina during the 1880s (as there are today): the conservatives who were reactionary against black progress and self-determination, and the liberals who sought to bring about a positive change in race relations. Each side has had its spokesman about the life and works of John Chavis. It will be left to posterity to decide which writers tried to present the facts and which the mythology.

The "Christopher" interview emphasizes Chavis's teaching mainly white children and preaching to white congregations; his excellent educational background as a classical scholar; and the blackness of his complexion along with the immaculateness of his dress. The article has a suspicious aura due to the anonymity of the interviewer and "Christopher." Also it is curious how the friendship with Dr. McPheeters is emphasized.

The Rev. Dr. Charles Phillips of Chapel Hill undertook the collection of data on John Chavis in 1883. He wrote letters to the sons of former students of John Chavis, asking for information about him. Paul Cameron wrote from Hillsboro, North Carolina:

> In my boyhood life at my Father's home, I often saw
> John Chavers a venerable old Negro man recognized as a
> free man and as a Preacher or Clergyman of the Presbyterian Church. As such he was received by my father and

> treated with kindness and consideration and respected by
> him as a man of education, good sense and most estimable
> character. He often called at ... my Father's residence 18
> miles East of Hillsboro. The manner of his reception con-
> vinced me that he had the confidence, respect and good will
> of his good friend Judge Cameron, while it excited the
> wonder of the tenants and slaves to see one of their race
> and color so pleasantly received and seated by their Master
> engaged in animated conversation.[5]

This description indicates the deference and social amenities which were extended to Chavis by his white associates and former pupils.

In his letter Mr. Cameron thought Chavis was a bachelor. He further describes him as being corpulent, 5 feet 6 or 7 inches in height, and always neat in appearance with his black homespun suit. He was further described as a "remarkable old Negro man with short and kinky hair and black skin."

Other questions which have concerned writers pertain to his marriage, children, and descendants. On May 18, 1883, Dr. Phillips received a letter from G. W. Kittrell of Tally Ho, North Carolina. Captain J. H. Webb had asked Mr. Kittrell to write the letter for him. Mr. Kittrell writes,

> I ... will tell you what little I know of the late John
> Chavis. I think from the family connection that he was a
> native of N.C. belonged to the old issue of coloured peo-
> ple, was not black, between black and yellow, thick
> inclined to be a little fleshy, a very dignified gently looking
> man—was retiring did not put himself with white people.[6]

Here for the first time in writing is a somewhat different description of Chavis, showing that he might have been of mixed parentage.

Colonel George Wortham writes to attorney John H. Webb a very detailed account of John Chavis on May 22, 1883, from Oxford, N.C., regarding Chavis's appearance among other subjects:

> Mr. Chavis was of pure African blood. You know there
> are two distinct races of Negroes, the one black with low
> retreating forehead, flat nose and wanting in intelligence,
> the other brown with good cranial development and nose
> and lips approaching somewhat of the Caucasian type of
> much greater intelligence than the coal black race of

Negroes. Mr. Chavis was of a brown complexion, but evidently without any of the mixture of white blood in his veins.[7]

Wortham's description shows the influence of the racist ideologues of the nineteenth century, such as Gobineau, who claimed that one could tell the intelligence of a person by the shape of the head and other facial features.[8] This ideology was exploited by the pro-slavery apologists who tried to justify slavery on the basis of purported natural inferiority. Wortham's judgment of Chavis's physical appearance from this racist dogma clouded his perception. Of course within all races there are different types of physiognomies, but to tag inferiority upon one or another is absurd. How did Wortham know that Chavis was "of pure African blood"? The idea of a pure race is very subjective.

As to Chavis's birth, Wortham believes that "he was probably born in North Carolina in the grounds of Grassy Creek, Nutbush or Shiloh churches and was sent thence to Princeton, N. J." This conjecture seems feasible since Nutbush (in the present Townsville) and Grassy Creek (in the present Stovall) were founded before Chavis's birth in 1763. The Nutbush Presbyterian Church was established in 1757, according to a bronze tablet on the front. However a formal organization of the church did not occur until 1765 or 1766.[9] Grassy Creek Presbyterian Church was organized a year or two after Nutbush. The United States Census indicates that Chavises were living in both of these areas at that time.

In spite of some of the racist sounding remarks, the importance of Wortham's letter is that some of his conjectures coincide with the Chavis family's oral tradition and history. Wortham writes:

> He had married and died sometime about 1845 to 1850 at the house of Martin Chavis, a worthy and well to do millwright—six miles north of Oxford. Martin Chavis was a relation of Rev. John Chavis and I think was a grandson or son-in-law or something of that kind of Mr. Chavis. He (Mr. Chavis) must have been some seventy five or eighty years old at his death. He was supported partly by Martin Chavis, partly by an allowance made him by Orange Presbytery ... and partly by voluntary contributions made him by his former pupils and his other friends.[10]

It is true that Rev. Chavis was married at the time of his death.

However, the dates of 1845 to 1850 are much later than the date of 1838 that is given by succeeding historians. The name *Martin* Chavis is a mis-interpretation of *Mark* Chavis. There is no reference to Martin Chavis in the censuses of Granville, Wake, Franklin or Orange counties. Mark Chavis was the brother of John Chavis. He is listed in the tax list of Granville County for 1820. When John was unable to preach or teach because of the restrictions imposed after the Nat Turner insurrection of 1831, Mark undertook partial support of his brother. He also supported his sister-in-law Frances after the death of his brother.

Mr. J. H. Horner, the founder of Horner Military Academy in Oxford, states that Chavis died in Granville County near the Wake County line about 1840. He reports that "Col. Amis saw him old and feeble in 1838." About Chavis's appearance, Horner reports,

> When a small boy I saw Chavis at my father's house. I have a very distinct memory of his personal appearance. He was then advanced in years but had no wrinkles, He was stout and corpulent with full large round face and of a brilliant color—quite black, but it was not a dingy or smutty black. His personal appearance was dignified and calculated to command respect.[11]

This description somewhat coincides with Wortham's description.

Dr. Kemp P. Battle, president of the University of North Carolina at Chapel Hill, wrote to Mr. Edward Oldham on May 27, 1889, from Chapel Hill. He stated that "Chavis (or Chaves) was an excellent man," and that the Honorable Paul C. Cameron of Raleigh could provide him with facts about Chavis. Dr. Battle suggested questions which Mr. Oldham might ask, which are still germane today:

1. Where did Chaves teach?
2. When did Chaves teach?
3. Name some of his pupils.
4. What was his color, i.e. how much white blood?
5. Did he teach Latin or Greek?
6. Algebra?
7. Did he leave descendants and are they prosperous and worthy?

While he might not be willing to write a broadcast letter, I think he will answer your questions.[12]

Clearly, Chavis's life story has inspired many researchers to pursue information that could lead to a clearer picture of the man—beginning, perhaps, with his genealogy. The Chavis Family of Oxford, North Carolina, and Granville County is a part of one of the largest families in North Carolina, stretching from the shores of Ocracoke Sounds in the East to the Blue Ridge Mountains in the West. The name Chavis originates from the Spanish surname Chavez, which was given to a great number of American Indians by a Spanish conquistador of that surname in the 1400s when the Spaniards were conquering parts

John, Lord Carteret, First Earl of Granville

of North America, Central America, and South America. The name Chavez originates from a Portuguese coat of arms. When the English came in contact with the Indians, the name was changed from Chavez to Chavis. These were Cherokee Indians for the most part. Like the Spaniards, they intermarried and mixed with their African companions, servants and slaves.

Granville County during the early eighteenth century was claimed by the Earl of Granville (John, Lord Carteret) as his own, and he subsequently granted deeds to white settlers as well as to Indians who were already residing in what later was called southern Virginia and northern Granville County. The Earl of Granville was secretary of state to King George II.

In the Granville County branch of the Chavis family, the oldest known relatives are ten generations from the present generation. Gibrea Chavis, a Cherokee Indian and the son of Bartholomew Chavis, married Ann Priddy, a Caucasian, daughter of Robert Priddy, in the eighteenth century.[13]

Gibrea Chavis had come to Granville County in the northern part

This Indenture Made the ___ Day of ___ in the Year of our Lord One Thousand Seven Hundred and ___ Between the Right Honourable John Earl Granville, Viscount Carteret and Baron Carteret, of Hawnes in the County of Bedford, in the Kingdom of Great-Britain, Lord President of his Majesty's Most Honourable Privy Council, and Knight of the Most Noble Order of the Garter, of the one Part; and ___ of the other Part. WHEREAS His Most Excellent Majesty King George the Second, in the Eighteenth Year of his Reign, and in the Year of our Lord One Thousand Seven Hundred and Forty Four, and made between His said Most Excellent Majesty of the one Part, and the said John Earl Granville, by the Name, Stile and Title, of the Right Honourable John Lord Carteret, of the other Part; DID, for the Considerations therein-mentioned, Give and Grant, Release, Ratify and Confirm, unto the said Earl, (by the Name, Stile and Title, of John Lord Carteret, as aforesaid) and his Heirs and Assigns, for ever, a certain District, Territory, or Parcel of Land, lying in the Province of North-Carolina in America, and all the Sounds, Creeks, Havens, Ports, Rivers, Streams, and other Royalties, Franchises, Privileges and Immunities, within the same, as they are therein set out, or described, to the said John Earl Granville, as aforesaid; for one Eighth Part of the Charters granted by King Charles the Second, in the Fifteenth and Seventeenth Years of his Reign to Eight Lords Proprietors of Carolina; as by the said Indenture duly Enrolled in the High Court of Chancery in Great-Britain, and in the Secretary's Office of the Province of North-Carolina, Reference being thereunto had, will more fully appear. Now THIS INDENTURE WITNESSETH, That as well for and in Consideration of the Sum of Ten Shillings Sterling Money to the said John Earl Granville in Hand paid, by the said ___ at or before the Sealing and Delivery of these Presents, the Receipt whereof he the said Earl doth hereby acknowledge; as also for and in Consideration of the ___ yearly Rent hereinafter reserved and contained, and by and on the Part and Behalf of the said ___ Heirs and Assigns, for ever, ALL that Tract or Parcel of vacant Land, situate, lying and being, in the County of ___

Containing in the Whole, ___ Acres of Land; all which Premises are more particularly described and set forth in the Plan or Map thereof hereunto annexed; TOGETHER with all Woods, Underwoods, Timber-Trees, Water-Courses, and the Privilege of Hunting, Hawking, Fishing and Fowling, in and upon the Premises, and all Mines and Minerals whatsoever therein to be found, (excepting, and always reserving out of this present Grant unto the King's Most Excellent Majesty, His Heirs and Successors, one Fourth Part of all the Gold and Silver Mines to be found in and upon the Premises; and also EXCEPTING, and always reserving unto the said John Earl Granville, his Heirs and Assigns, one Moiety or Half Part of the remaining Three Fourths of all such Gold and Silver Mines;) To HAVE AND TO HOLD the said Tract or Parcel of vacant Land, and all and singular other the Premises with their Appurtenances, (except before excepted,) unto the said ___ Heirs and Assigns, for ever; YIELDING AND PAYING therefore Yearly, and every Year, unto the said John Earl Granville, his Heirs or Assigns, the Yearly Rent or Sum of ___ which is at the Rate of Three Shillings Sterling for every Hundred Acres, and (so in Proportion for a less Quantity, at or upon the Twenty-fifth Day of March, and the Twenty-ninth Day of September in every Year, by even and equal Portions, and to be paid at the Court-House of the said County of ___ unto the said Earl, his Heirs or Assigns, or to his or their lawful Attorney or Receiver for the Time being, the first Payment thereof to be made or the aforementioned Days of Payment, as shall first happen after the Date thereof. AND the said ___ for ___ Heirs and Assigns, and to and with either and every of them, by these Presents, in Manner and Form following ; That is to say, That ___ Heirs and Assigns, shall and will Yearly, and for every Year for ever, well and truly pay or cause to be paid unto the said Earl, his Heirs or Assigns, the aforesaid Yearly Rent or Sum of ___ or any Part thereof, shall, at any Time hereafter, be behind or unpaid for the Space of Six Months, next over or after either of the aforementioned Days of Payment, (and no sufficient Distress can be found on the Premises whereon it shall be lawful to levy such Rents and Arrears, with the full Costs, Charges and Expences, in making the same) That then this present Grant, and all Assignment thereof, shall be utterly void and of none Effect : And it shall be lawful for the said Earl, his Heirs or Assigns, to reenter into the said Lands, and to regrant the same to any other Person or Persons whomsoever, as if this Grant, and such Assignments, had never been made. IN WITNESS whereof, the Parties above-named have to these Presents interchangeably set their Hands and Seals, the Day and Year herein first above-written.

Sealed and Delivered
  in the Presence of

of North Carolina from Virginia by way of the eastern counties. He was the brother of William Chavis, who is classified in the early census as a Negro, indicating that his mother was an African. Gibrea had three sons, all mulattos: William, James, and Jacob. William had two sons, William and Phillip. Gibrea lived in Williamsboro, which was at one time a part of Granville County and Old Bute County. (Now it is a part of Vance County.) Having a princely estate of thousands of acres given to him by the Earl of Granville himself, Gibrea entertained himself like the other farmers in that section of the woods by hunting, fishing, and horse racing. His beautiful stallion "Black Snake" was the best horse in the races at Williamsboro. Gibrea taught his sons how to farm, to raise cattle and horses. They also taught themselves how to read and write. Their education per-

Land plat attached to the land grant from the Earl of Granville to Phillip Chavis, 1761. The plat included the acreage and a description of the land. (North Carolina Division of Archives and History, Raleigh.)

haps was an inspiration to Gibrea's great-great grandson, John Chavis, who would be the first black minister ordained in the Presbyterian Church, would attend Princeton University, and would prepare the sons of the white gentry in English, Greek, and Latin so that they could attend the University of North Carolina at Chapel Hill, which was in the formulative stage.

In 1761, William's son Phillip was granted 700 acres of land "lying in Granville County on both sides of Buffalo Creek." Granville County was formed in 1746 and several counties were subsequently

Opposite page: Land grant from the Earl of Granville to Phillip Chavis, 1761. (North Carolina Division of Archives and History, Raleigh.)

carved from Granville: parts of Orange in 1752; parts of Johnston and Bladen in 1753; Bute in 1764; Warren in 1786; parts of Person in 1871; parts of Franklin in 1873 and 1875. Vance County was formed from Bute County, which had been a part of Granville, in 1881. Wake County was formed from Franklin County in 1771, which was carved from Granville County. A great portion of the land which was taken from Granville County at one time belonged to the Chavis family. The city of Louisburg is located on Buffalo Creek, the site of part of Phillip's land.

There was a Chavis Mill located in the vicinity of Williamsboro in the eighteenth and nineteenth centuries which was run by Mark Chavis.[14]

We have already seen evidence of conjecture about Chavis's place of birth and his family. Kittrell indicates that he was a native of North Carolina; Wortham believes he was born in Granville County, North Carolina, in the vicinity of Grassy Creek, Nutbush, or Shiloh church, and further indicates Chavis's relation to "Martin" (Mark) Chavis. Edgar W. Knight in his excellent study of John Chavis refers to the assertion put forth by W. H. Quick (*Negro Stars in All Ages of the World*), Edward A. Johnson (*A School History of the Negro Race in America*), and J. L. Seawell (*Black Teacher of Southern Whites*) that John Chavis came from the West Indian Islands.[15] According to Knight, "Johnson says that 'This gentleman ... came to the United States in 1822.'" This date is not correct because Chavis said of himself in a letter to Willie P. Mangum, "If I am Black, I am a free born American and a revolutionary soldier."[16]

A number of historians, including John Spencer Bassett,[17] Charles Lee Smith,[18] and G. C. Shaw,[19] accord Chavis a Granville County, North Carolina, origin. According to Knight, Smith believed that "he was born near Oxford in Granville County." Bassett says, "He was, probably, born in Granville County, near Oxford, about 1763." According to Barbara Parramore,[20] a court record in the form of a certificate made in 1802 showing Chavis's completion of a "regular course of study at Washington Academy in Rockbridge County," Virginia, indicates that he was 40 years old at the time. This document confirms his birth in either 1762 or 1763.

Dr. G. C. Shaw also finds the Granville County origin of Chavis's birth to be more authentic. He interviewed an elderly lady in Granville County who confirmed this belief. She was a Mrs. Sarah Young, who stated:

Above, left: Dr. G. C. Shaw, Presbyterian minister and founder of Mary Potter High School in Oxford, North Carolina, the county seat of Granville County. *Above, right:* Mrs. Sarah Young, descendant of John Chavis, whom Dr. Shaw interviewed. (Both photographs from *John Chavis* by G. C. Shaw. Binghamton, NY: Vail-Ballou, 1932.)

> John Chavis was the son of my great-grandmother, Lottie Chavis. I've heard my mother and grandmother, Peggy Chavis, speak of him often, and my grandmother said he often visited and spent much time in her home.... My grandmother, mother and great grandmother were all free people and Presbyterians. [21]

An early census of Granville County shows Peg Chavis as a member of the household of Phillip Chavis (Chavers),[22] thus establishing the link between John Chavis and William, Gibrea and Phillip. Another authenticating record shows John Chavis as the bondsman at the marriage of Lottie Chavis (his mother) to Littleton Tabron on April 14, 1818.[23] Mrs. Young was at the time of the publication of Dr. Shaw's book was eighty-six years of age. Dr. Shaw believes that she was from a Presbyterian background because of her ability to read and write.

BARE [BEAR] SWAMP DISTRICT

Taxables	Masters & C.	Whites	Blacks; Free	Slaves, male (>16 yr)	Slaves, male (<16 yr)	Slaves, female	Total
1. James ROSS & son James							
Richard SMITH							
Burrell JONES	1	3	0	0	0	0	4
2. Richard CLAPTON							
James HARRIS							
*Jinne,*Tamer,*Hanner	1	1	0	1	0	0	3
*Sam,*Halman,							
3. John YARBROUGH							
Willm DANE							
*Tom	1	1	0	2	0	3	7
4. David GREEN	1	0	0	0	0	0	1
5. Jo.s STONE	1	0	0	0	0	0	1
6. Christipher JOHNSON & son Willm	1	1	0	0	0	0	2
7. Wm ANDERSON & son William	1	1	0	0	0	0	2
8. Willm WILLIFERD	1	0	0	0	0	0	1
9. George RICHARDS	1	0	0	0	0	0	1
10. James RAINWATER	1	0	0	0	0	0	1
11. Elisabeth OLIVER [not taxable]							
Jacob ADDAM							
Bennery NIXON	0	2	0	0	0	0	2
12. Browning WILLIAM & son John	1	1	0	0	0	0	2
13. Thos. BECKUM & son Willm	1	1	0	0	0	0	2
14. James PIERCE Oves.							
*Jack,*Cofe,*Ned,*Mingo							
*Hannah,*Nan	1	0	0	3	1	2	7
Willm RICHERSON	1	0	0	0	0	0	1
James CARREL & brother Delany CARRELL	1	1	0	0	0	0	2
MOONEY & son John	1	1	0	0	0	0	2
Willm HARRIS	1	0	0	0	0	0	1
Wm RUSSELL & son Willm	1	1	0	0	0	0	2
John RUSSELL	1	0	0	0	0	0	1
Phillip CHAVERS ✓							
Celea CHAVERS ✓							
*Pegg,*Parrot	0	0	2	0	0	2	4
Christipher CLERK	1	0	0	0	0	0	1
John CLARK	1	0	0	0	0	0	1
Paul PATRICK							
*Simon,*Jubiter,*Jinne	1	0	0	2	0	1	4
Jeremiah BROWN	1	0	0	0	0	0	1
Phillemon EDWARDS	1	0	0	0	0	0	1
Wm EAVES & sons Benj^a & Willm	1	2	0	0	0	0	3

No.	Taxables	Masters & C.	Whites	Blacks; Free	Slaves, male (>16 yr)	Slaves, male (<16 yr)	Slaves, female	Total
28.	Dan+ CARRELL & bros. Willm & Mark HARDEN	1	2	0	0	0	0	3
29.	John MASSE & sons John & William *Tabb & *Rachel	1	2	0	0	0	2	5
30.	Henry HILL Lamuel LANIER *Sam,*Bess,*Cary	1	1	0	1	1	1	5
31.	Zacharias YARBROUGH	1	0	0	0	0	0	1
32.	Manoah YARBROUGH David HUES	1	1	0	0	0	0	2
33.	Tho.s SHEARWOOD	1	0	0	0	0	0	1
34.	Francis MABRY & son Francis *Jack,*Patt	1	1	0	1	0	1	4
35.	Wm. Reiley DAVIS	1	0	0	0	0	0	1
36.	Joseph BRANTLY & son John	1	1	0	0	0	0	2
37.	Joshua YARBROUGH	1	0	0	0	0	0	1
38.	Tho.s WEST Cons. & son Tho.s	0	1	0	0	0	0	1
39.	Simon BECKUM	1	0	0	0	0	0	1
40.	Tho.s THARENTON	1	0	0	0	0	0	1
41.	Parson RACKLEY	1	0	0	0	0	0	1
42.	John FARMER	1	0	0	0	0	0	1
43.	John FIKE & sons John & Nathan	1	2	0	0	0	0	3
44.	Willm BALLARD	1	0	0	0	0	0	1
45.	Wm RICHARDS *Fillis	1	0	0	0	0	1	2
46.	John CARREL	1	0	0	0	0	0	1
47.	Thos. WOODLEY	1	0	0	0	0	0	1
48.	Joel WALKER *Ned	1	0	0	0	1	0	2
49.	John MURDOCK *Dave	1	0	0	0	1	0	2
50.	Jacob CROCKER	1	0	0	0	0	0	1
51.	Waddenton ABBIT & son Willm *Frank,*Mugraw,*Sarah	1	1	0	2	0	1	5
52.	John BURT & son John John BOWERS *Lilley,*Fillis	1	2	0	0	0	2	5
53.	John GUNN	1	0	0	0	0	0	1
54.	Giles BOWERS Nickless DILLIARD *Cloe	1	1	0	0	0	1	3
55.	Thos. SMITH & son Willm *Y. Peter,*Old Peter,*Jack, *Dinah,*Bett,*Luce	1	1	0	3	0	3	8

Taxables in the Bear Swamp District of Granville County in 1762. This list shows Peg Chavis as a member of the household of Phillip Chavis (Chavers). (From the *North Carolina Genealogical Society Journal* XII, no. 3 [August 1986].)

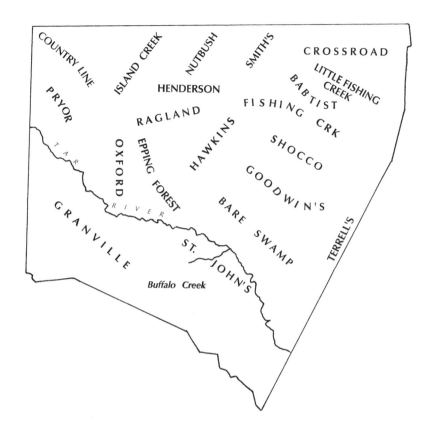

Granville County Tax District, 1762. Phillip Chavis owned land on both sides of Buffalo Creek in the Bare Swamp District. (From the *North Carolina Genealogical Journal* XII, no. 3 [August 1986].)

Shaw also felt that Rev. Chavis was born in Granville County, "about nine miles from Oxford at a locality known as 'Reavis Cross Roads.'" This is the same Reavis Crossroads where Chavis conducted his classical school.

As we can see from the discussion above, Chavis was descended from mixed heritage: African, Indian and Caucasian. He was indeed a remarkable man for his time, but from the perspective of the social and political atmosphere of this corner of North Carolina in the eighteenth century, one can understand how he came to be.

Granville county, which at that time bordered and in some sections still borders the state of Virginia, borrowed some of the characteristics of the neighboring state during the colonial period.

Virginia very early in the seventeenth century saw a blood mixture of Caucasians and Indians. Indians who intermarried with Caucasians were legally free. When Africans came to Virginia, there were at first some indentured servants who later paid for their freedom in much the same way as the Caucasians paid for theirs. The children of these free blacks were also free.

There were also instances of free Black men marrying Caucasian women. A well known case is Benjamin Banneker, whose mother was white and whose father was an African. The offspring of white women were legally free. Not only were the children of the free white women and the free black men legally free, but the children of the white masters were often set free at a certain age or at the master's will. Similarly, there were marriages among Africans, Caucasians, and Indians, creating blood ties. Even though records were kept of free blacks in Virginia as early as 1872, through natural increase there were thousands who were unaccounted for.[24]

There were also many runaway slaves, who sometimes were captured by Indians. According to Babcock, "Slaves had been running away a century and a half before the Revolution, but what in peacetime was a rivulet became a wartime flood."

There was much buying and selling of slaves between Mecklenburg County, Virginia, and Granville County, North Carolina. The practice of manumitting or freeing slaves came very early in Virginia. In 1790 in Mecklenburg County, there were "1,857 free White males 16 years and upwards; 2,016 free White males under 16; 3,683 free White females; 416 all other free persons, and 2,558 slaves."[25] McColley reveals that Virginians did not have a "consensus of opinion about slavery and manumission." Some Virginians opposed manumissions, especially of slaves with many children.[26]

The revolutionary fervor for freedom also resulted in the passage of manumission laws. According to McColley, "In May of 1782, shortly before the war was officially concluded by the Treaty of Paris, the Virginians passed a law allowing private manumissions." However, the instances of manumission created many legal problems, especially in regard to wills which had been probated naming slaves as heir property because it had been illegal to free slaves before 1782.*

*The House of Burgesses in April 1691 had passed a statute ordering "that no Negro or mulatto be after the end of the present session of the assembly, set free by person or persons whatsoever, unless such person or persons, their heirs, executors or administrators pay for the transportation of such Negroes out of the country within six months after setting them free." Ballagh, History of Slavery in Virginia, cites The Statutes of Virginia, Vol. 3, 87.

According to a study made in 1939, there were some seventeen different Indian tribes in the Tidewater area of Virginia and the Granville (North Carolina) area when the first white settlers penetrated it in the 1740s. Most numerous in the southern Virginia area and in Granville County were the Tuscaroras and the Cherokees.[27] As mentioned above, a name which many of the Tuscaroras and Cherokees took from the Spanish explorers and which the English settlers found them using was Chavez. As late as 1786 there was a Cezar Chavez in Bertie County.[28] During the eighteenth century, the name was changed to different variations: Chavis, Chavers, Cheves, Chavous, and Chavious. In the 1790 census William Chavis is listed in Mecklenburg County, Virginia, as well as in the Fishing Creek District of Granville County. James Chavis is listed in the Abraham Plains District of Granville County.

Wherever there were Chavises in Granville County, there were Caucasians, notably the Smiths, Roysters, Yanceys, Boyds, Milliners, Taylors, Satterwhites, Parrishes, Ridleys, Snellings, Thorpes, Persons, Beezleys, and Daniels. The northern European Caucasians came from Virginia and were Scotch Irish Presbyterians.[29]

It is to be noted that some of the Smiths who were very instrumental in seeing that the young John Chavis went to Princeton lived in Granville County. Samuel Smith, whose home was called Abraham Plains (after which the township was named), lived near James Chavis. Grassy Creek Church was located in this township and is near Satterwhite, the home of John Chavis's relatives and some of his descendants. Some Smiths also lived in the Fishing Creek Township of Granville County, the location of William Chavis's large plantation. There were Benjamin Smith and Henry Smith.[30]

The Cherokee Indians had long familiarity with the Caucasians since the coming of the Spanish in the sixteenth century. They would later act as guides and interpreters for the English. Many of those who converted to Christianity took Christian names. It is interesting that many of the Cherokees and Tuscaroras who intermarried with or were the children of mixed parentage were named Isham or Ishmael after the outcast son of Abraham (by Hagar) described in the book of Genesis.

In time many of the Cherokees adopted the ways of the white man in regard to slavery for economic and political purposes. Perhaps in order to coexist with the invaders it was necessary to adopt their ways. The Cherokees already had their own institutions of servitude, but the slaves which they had kept before the Europeans' arrival were war captives. These slaves were not treated as non-humans or "three-fifths of a man." According to Perdue, "The Cherokees accorded the same privileges to war prisoners who had married or were adopted into the tribe as they did to those whose membership derived from birth, and adopted captives were reluctant to leave the Cherokees."[31]

With the introduction of African slavery during the nineteenth century on a wholesale basis, many Cherokees engaged in the trade for economic purposes. There were many instances when they stole slaves from whites. However, many Cherokees were governed by their traditional humane treatment of captives in the institution of slavery. (Others, according to Siler, especially many of the half breeds, were not compassionate to their slaves.[32]) After the passing of time, the mixed children of Indian women and enslaved men became "free issues," exercising all of the privileges of the free people.

There is a tradition among the Chavises that they have always been free. However, in the distant past some of the Chavis African ancestors were held in slavery or some type of servitude. Perdue explains that for the most part the Cherokees did not like to refer to their servants as slaves but as brothers.[33]

Many of the areas in which John Chavis lived during his lifetime, although then considered to be a part of Granville County, are now called by other county names. Because of its expansive size, several counties were formed from Granville.[34] As mentioned above, Wake County was formed in 1771 from parts of Franklin County which had formerly been a part of Granville County.

David Corbit gives the following history:

> Granville County was formed in 1746 from Edgecombe. It was named in honor of John Carteret, Earl of Granville, who owned the Granville District.... It is in the northeastern section of the state and is bounded by Vance, Franklin, Wake, Durham, and Person counties and the state of Virginia. The present area is 543 square miles and the population is 29,347.[35]

William Chavis, the grandfather of John Chavis, owned thousands of acres of land in Granville County, which he had inherited from his father, Bartholomew Chavis. Hundreds of acres of his land were later sold to white settlers. Later he received land from them.[36]

William Chavis had also been granted lands by the Earl of Granville (Granville County Grantees, Book H 457). William Chavis's deed from the Earl of Granville granted him "all of the land from Collins Creek and Tar River to the County line." Phillip Chavis inherited the lands from his father, William. Phillip also received a land grant from the Earl of Granville on the 29th of July 1761.

Gibrea Chavis died in 1777. On January 5, 1778, Ann Chavis, the daughter of Robert Priddy (Caucasian) and widow of Gibrea Chavis (Cherokee Indian), was assigned her dower in the land, "150 acres on Boiling Spring Branch to Long Creek."[37] Gibrea's brother William died February 5, 1777 (the same year as Gibrea), and William's son Phillip Chavis rendered an inventory of the estate during the February court of 1778.[38] By November 21, 1778, Phillip Chavis had sold 220 acres of his land to Caucasian Richard Clopton. These acres of land then passed from the Cloptons to Jonathan Davis in a deed dated 23 February 1811.[39] It is worth noting that the name of John Chavis is written on the back of these deeds, which are housed in the North Carolina Archives. (See Appendix A for facsimiles of relevant documents).

Attorney Thomas Person, surveyor of Granville County and the largest landowner (30,000 acres), was appointed guardian of Jesse Chavis, another son of William Chavis.

Phillip Chavis was married to Celea Chavis. They lived in the Bear Swamp area of Granville County. Phillip had two children, Peggy (sic) and Parrot, living with him.[40] We recall that Mrs. Sarah Young had told Dr. G. C. Shaw that her grandmother, Peggy Chavis, had told her that John Chavis was the son of Sarah's great grandmother, Lottie Chavis. It is possible that Peggy, the daughter of Phillip's son William and Lottie Chavis, was living with Phillip Chavis, her grandfather. Being the daughter of Lottie, she was also sister of John Chavis.

By the 1830s William Chavis, father of John Chavis, was living in the city of Raleigh, "east of Fayetteville and Halifax Streets."[41] Phillip's wife Celea and her relatives Rachel, Charity, Jane and Lidia were living in the St. Matthew's District of Raleigh, where Oakwood Avenue and the Oakwood district are located today.[42] As mentioned earlier, Gibrea Chavis (sometimes called Gibson Chavis or Chavers) and William Chavis (sometimes spelled Chavers) owned land in Mecklenburg County, Virginia (adjoining Granville County), as well as in Granville County. Descendants of the Chavises were still living in Mecklenburg County, Virginia, in 1830.[43]

Granville County ss.

Know all men by these presents that we Thomas Person, Thos. Tatter
and ... ile & ... Benj.... of the said County are held and firmly bound unto
John Paw...
Thomas Person Esquire a Justice of the said County Court of Granville in the
Sum of Hundred ...... Proclamation Money to be paid to said Thos. Person
Esquire or to his Successors to which payment well and truly to be made we bind our
Selves and each of our heirs &c. jointly and Severally firmly by these presents Sealed
with our seals and dated this 9 day Augt Anno. Domi. 1780

The Condition of this Obligation is such that whereas the above bound ——
.... at a Court held for the said County the day of the date of these presents
was Nominated and appointed Guardian of Jesse Chavis orphan of
Wm Chavis Deceased and was by virtue thereof, impowered and authoriz'd to
take into his Custody and possession all the estate Right, Property and Interest
whatsoever and wheresoever to be found of him the said ... within
the said County. Now if the the said Thos. Person his heirs Executors or Ad-
-ministrators shall and do Render a Just true and perfect Account of all the estate
goods and Chattels Rights and Profits belonging to the said Jesse Chavis
as shall come into his hands possessions knowledge or the hands or possession if any
other person or persons whatsoever by himself or his procurement and the same on
oath do Exhibit to the Justices or their Successors in open Court within Three months
from the date hereof to be entered on the Records of the said Court and Deliver
to the said Jesse Chavis when and as soon as he shall arrive at the
age of Twenty one years in kind, quantity and quality pursuant to the Laws
of this State in that Case made and provided and shall save harmless and
Indemnify'd the said John Paw Esqr from and concerning any
Estate of the Justices of the said & Jesse Chavis and also shall at
any time when Required by the Justices of the said Court or their Successors

Carried over

Here and facing page: Guardian bond to Thomas Person granting him guardianship over "Jesse" Chavis, son of William Chaivs, 1780. (North Carolina Division of Archives and History, Raleigh.)

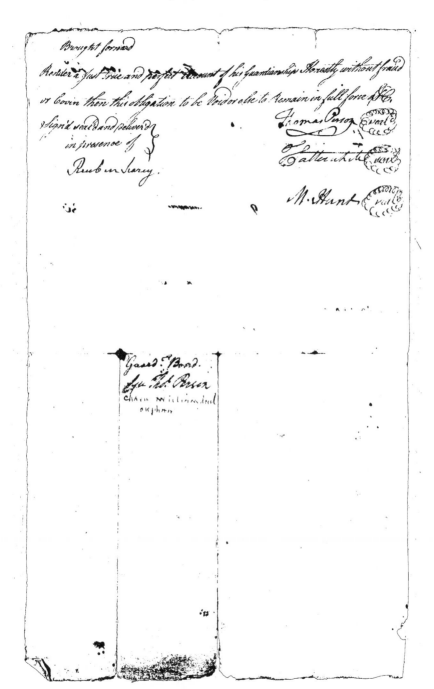

O. W. Blacknall in an article dated October 31, 1895, discusses the Chavises:

> I also confounded two generations of Chavises. The large land owner was William Chavis. All the farms here about, large and small, were carved from the Old Chavis tract. This tract began at Lynch's creek, between Kittrell and Louisburg, and ran, with a breadth of about five miles, sixteen miles up the north bank of Tar river to Fishing creek near Oxford.[44]

The wide expanse of William Chavis's land is further documented by S. T. Peace.[45] William Chavis had lived in old Bute County (where Fishing Creek rises), the county which later became Vance County. Peace describes a road that seems to be interminable called Chaves (sic) Road, leading from Kittrell into Granville County. It seems that O. W. Blacknall, the writer of the *News and Observer* article, may be related to the C. L. Blacknall, an elderly man and repository of Vance County's history, whom Peace alludes to in his study. O. W. Blacknall further states:

> As Chavis began alienating the land before the revolution there is every reason to believe that he had it direct from the Lord Granville, one of the Lord Proprietors who instead of receding his interest in the Carolinas to the Crown as the others did, took a princely domain comprising this part of the State. The facts that Chavis land was so large and bounded by well known water courses tend to confirm this belief.[46]

Blacknall is correct in the above statement, but he confuses Gibrea Chavis with his nephew John Chavis:

> The handwriting of William Chavis indicates an educated man. But I find that *it was one of his sons*, probably Gibbs Chavis, that was the school teacher and taught white children [*The News and Observer*, Thursday, October 31, 1895].

The following account by Blacknall tells of the mysterious death of either William Chavis, Gibrea Chavis or John Chavis:

> Gibbs Chavis—I am not sure that he was the school teacher, he might have been his brother—was a great horse

racer. His horse, Black Snake, had no equal in his day and won his owner a great deal of money, and was finally the cause of his death. At a great race up near a stream still known as Gibbs' Creek, Black Snake's running bankrupted the crowd as usual. Bad blood was engendered. A quarrel arose. On the way home, in the dark, Chavis was shot and killed [*The News and Observer*, Thursday, October 31, 1895].

Blacknall's next statement confirms the fact that John Chavis was almost certainly born in Granville County and that his descendants still live there.

The Presbyterian minister, Chavis of whom Mr. Winston speaks, was probably a son or descendant of the original William Chavis. Many of his descendants live.... Few or any of them even know that the family ever saw better days.

Blacknall goes on:

An investigation as far as practicable of their genealogy showed them to be largely of Indian blood. This was fully confirmed by their features and physical structure. Among, them, especially among their women, the Indian character-istics are strongly marked. I know of more than one who could easily pass for an Indian squaw.

The Chavises and the Harrises were the first African and mixed breed African-Americans to be recognized as free persons in Granville County, North Carolina. They are listed among the earli-est inhabitants of the county.

During the colonial period companies were organized under the leadership of captains to protect the various settlements. According to Worth S. Ray:

Authentic copy of the master roll of a regiment of militia under the command of Colonel William Eaton, as taken at a general muster of said regiment on October 8, 1754, as shown on pages 370 to 380 inclusive, of Volume 22, of the North Carolina State Records, including the names of both officers and men

William Eaton   Colonel
William Person   Lieut. Colonel
James Paine   Major

The Regiment consisted of eight companies, in command
of the following Captains:

1. Capt. John Glover   97 men
2. Capt. George Jeffrey   83 men
3. Capt. Richard Coleman   94 men
4. Capt. Daniel Harris   95 men
5. Capt. John Sallis   90 men
6. Capt. Sugar Jones   140 men
7. Capt. Benjamin Simms   75 men
8. Capt. Andrew Hampton   60 men

The total number of men, exclusive of the Commissioned
officers of the Regiment and the companies was 734, and
the entire personnel of the regiment probably represented
every able bodied male person, subject to military duty at
that time (1754) residing within the bounds of Colonial
Granville County as shown on the Searcy, and the accom-
panying sketched map.[47]

Within Captain John Glover's company are listed William
Chavers, Negro; William Chavers, Jr., Mulatto; Gilbert Chavers,
Mulatto; and Edward Harris, Negro. The fact that William Chavis
is listed as a Negro indicates that his mother was an African. How-
ever, William married a Caucasian and therefore his sons William,
Jr., and Gilbert were mulattos.

In the list of Taxpayers of Granville County for the year of
1788—"which was used by the Federal Government as a substitute
for the first census of 1790"—are listed James Blackwell of Fishing
Creek District, William Chavers (Chavis) of Fishing Creek District,
James Chavis of Abraham Plains District, John Clement of Knap of
Leeds District, James Downey of Abraham Plains District, and
Edward Harris of Beaver Dam District.[48] This record of 1788 shows
that the population of free people of color in Granville County had
grown substantially within a period of thirty years.

In the meantime verification exists that Gibrea Chavis was the
father of William Chavis. In a will of the fourth day of January,
1777, Gibrea Chavis wrote:

> [I] Gibrea Chavis ... bequeath unto my son William
> Chavis all my land and plantation whereon I now live his
> heirs and assigns forever. To my wife Nanny one horse
> called Brittain and two cows and calves, four sows and
> pigs, one feather bed and furniture and all my pewter
> knives and forks during her natural life and widowhood.

I will that all the rest of my lands, goods & chattels be sold and after my debts & funeral charges be paid that the remainder be given to my son William his heirs and assigns forever and likewise that I have given to my wife after her death or marriage be given to my son William, his heirs and assigns forever. I will that my spotted mare be left for use of the plantation. Lastly, I do make and ordain my friends John Peace Senn, and John Kittrell executors of this my last will and testament dated this fourth day of January 1777.

Witnesses

Aquila Snelling

X

Joseph Peace

E

Elener Chavis[49]

As free blacks, the Chavises participated in all of the wars in defense of America's heritage and freedom. As shown above, the earliest known ancestors were militia men during the colonial period. John Chavis and other Chavises from Mecklenburg County, Virginia, and Orange County, North Carolina, participated in the Revolutionary War, as will be seen in the next chapter concerning the education and early years of John Chavis.

Therefore the evidence is strong that John Chavis was indeed a native of Granville County, North Carolina, and that he descended from the early settlers Gibrea Chavis and William Chavis.

There is still much conjecture over John Chavis's birthplace, whether in Mecklenburg County, Virginia, according to Madrue Chavers[50] and Daniel L. Boyd[51]; the Old Providence area of Granville County according to Elizabeth Murray[52] and Edgar Knight's "Notes on John Chavis"[53]; or Reavis Crossroads in Granville County.[54] It appears with all probability that John Chavis was reared in the Abraham Plains District, and this reference is made by George Wortham in his letter to Dr. Phillips quoted above. This was the area in which Grassy Creek Church was founded. Also the powerful Samuel Smith of the Presbyterian faith lived in this area. He was perhaps one of the sponsors who helped Chavis go to Princeton. As mentioned earlier, the township of Abraham Plains is named after Smith's home.[55] James Chavis, an ancestor of John Chavis, also lived in the Abraham Plains section. An interesting discovery during the research for this book was that relatives of James Milner, to whom John Chavis as a lad is believed to have been an indentured servant, lived in the Abraham Plains section. Before Samuel Smith moved there, this district was known as the County Line district. There was a James Milner living in this district in the 1780s. [56] The elder James Milner's connection with John Chavis is discussed in the next chapter. The possibility of Chavis's being an indentured servant of James Milner of Halifax County was first discussed by Barbara Parramore.[57]

Therefore the official records and the oral history document that John Chavis was born and reared in Granville County, North Carolina, probably until he became an indentured servant of James Milner of Halifax County, North Carolina.

It is further possible that he was born in the Bear Swamp District of Granville County, as it was called in 1762. This area is now a part of Franklin County, where the town of Louisburg is located. Louisburg is situated on Buffalo Creek, which was owned at that time by Chavis's ancestors.

It is also possible that John Chavis was born in Reavis Crossroads. The location of Reavis Crossroads is still being investigated. It perhaps has a different name today and is located either in Franklin County, Granville County or Wake County near Rogers store. Dr. Shaw states most assuredly:

> I feel sure that Mr. Chavis was born in Granville County and was a free man. About nine miles from Oxford there is a locality known as "Reavis' Crossroads." It is near this place that authentic tradition places Chavis' birth. He was free born, as Mrs. Young and her grandparents were: Near this section lived another historic family of free people, Tom Blackwell, whose son, John Blackwell, was very well known by my family. I have visited his home often and have known the direct descendants of Tom Blackwell practically all my life. He owned several slaves and more than a thousand acres of land. Much of the land is still owned by his descendants. He lived in a section known as "White Hall".... John Chavis, as I have said, was born at "Reavis' Crossroads," about ten miles from the home of Tom Blackwell and about nine miles southeast of Oxford.[58]

Many parallels exist between John Chavis's life and that of Dr. Shaw. Both were Presbyterian ministers, educators and Princeton University students. Dr. Shaw presents an erudite encomium to Chavis's birthplace and early life: "It matters but little, it is true, where or how a man is born so long as he proves to be a man."

CHAPTER 2

A Classical Education: A Black Man Drinks Deep of the Pierian Spring

John Chavis, according to Dr. Shaw, lived very near to "White Hall," the Presbyterian settlement of free blacks. Tom Blackwell, the principal land owner of the area, could read and write. Shaw believes that Blackwell not only influenced Chavis and his family to be educated, but "Tom Blackwell ... urged all free people to educate their *children.*"[1] Furthermore because of the prominence of John Chavis's own family as shown in the preceding chapter, it is also possible that not only Blackwell but Chavis's family encouraged him to attend school. The wills of Gibrea, William and Phillip Chavis are all signed in their own handwriting, indicating that they could read and write.

Another record of an environment which might have contributed to the educational background of John Chavis was a will of James Milner of Halifax, North Carolina, in the year 1773. This will shows that Milner owned a very large plantation, and most significantly, one of the richest personal libraries in the South. These facts were first revealed by Barbara Parramore in the *Dictionary of North Carolina Biography.*[2] If Parramore's information is truly about the same John Chavis of this study, they suggest reasons for his interest in, and success with, his education at Princeton University. James Milner bequeathed in his will of 1773 a large number of his books to Reverend William Willie of Sussex County, Virginia. According to Parramore,

> Milner, whose private library was one of the best and largest in North Carolina, was closely connected with the Mangum, Willie, and Jones families of Sussex County, Va.,

where he appears to have lived before coming to Halifax in
about 1766. The Reverend William Willie of Sussex, whose
surname was preserved in the branches of the Mangum and
Jones families and who moved to North Carolina, was the
beneficiary of the Greek and Latin volumes in Milner's
estate and may have played a role in Chavis's training and
education after Milner's death.[3]

No conclusive evidence has been found that Rev. Willie contributed to John Chavis's education, but the remarkable fact about
Parramore's finding is that she discovered in the inventory of Milner's estate (probated the 17th of December, 1773), the name of an
indentured servant named Jn. Chavis. This name is simply listed
among Milner's other property: "1 Portmanteau Trunk, 1 Observa-
tion on Gardening, 1 Indentured Servant named Jn. Chavis, 1 Laws
of No Carolina to 1765."[4] During the colonial period the court
ordered prominent men to provide for orphans and illegitimate children. They were ordered to make these children apprentices of master craftsmen or indentured servants who would serve and learn from
their "masters" for a period of time.[5]

Milner must have been a renaissance man, who sought knowledge about every subject imaginable. His library included volumes
on literary criticism, philosophy, farming, animal breeding, anatomy,
theology, linguistics, law, bookkeeping, poetry, literature, music,
mathematics, science, astronomy, political science, history, geography, and surveying, among many other subjects. If Rev. John Chavis
had been surrounded by this rich array of books as a young boy, he
perhaps became literate and a lover of learning at a very early age.
If we take the traditional date of his birth as 1763, he would have
been only ten years old at the time the inventory was taken.

As mentioned earlier, there was also a James Milliner (Milner)
mentioned in the 1786 Census of North Carolina in the County Line
district of Granville County, which was later called the Abraham
Plains district. This Milner might have been a relative of the elder
James Milner. The Abraham Plains district is near Satterwhite, the
ancestral home of the Chavises.

Like many of the Northern Europeans who migrated into
Granville and Halifax counties in the eighteenth century, attorney
James Milner was from Virginia. He also was probably a Presbyterian as were many of the early settlers. Dr. Samuel Smith Downey
records:

Presbyterianism, a rapidly spreading Protestant faith in the South, had grown under the powerful influence of Reverend Samuel Davies (1723–1760), a late, well-educated Calvinist clergyman, who resided in Hanover County, Virginia, for many years. He gleaned converts from the older ... Anglican establishment; these zealous people sought out homes in a neighboring colony [Granville County, North Carolina] where religious persecution was less tumultuous than that which had been waged in the Old Dominion.[6]

The Presbyterian colonists first settled in a section of Granville County known as Nutbush. Samuel T. Peace describes this area (which would later be part of Vance County) as follows:

Beginning with Williamsboro, which was in Nut Bush territory and at one time called Nut Bush, and extending to the Virginia line was part of Vance County (once Granville) called Nut Bush. It includes all the north end of the county and not just the small part included today in Nut Bush Township. The name is taken from the old Nut Bush Creek which rises in Henderson and flows north in the Roanoke River.[7]

Even before the Hanover Presbytery (which has jurisdiction over the southern states) was organized in 1755, Presbyterians were in Granville County, according to Downey's study. The Nutbush Presbyterian Church was formed in 1765 or 1767, followed by Grassy Creek and Lower Hyco. The Reverend James Creswell became, in 1764, "their first full-time minister."[8] According to Peace,

In the Hanover "Minutes," the Grassy Creek and Nutbush congregations are noted individually by names, 25 January 1758; from thence until early 1761, these congregations were constantly appealing for the services of an approved person. In April of the latter year, the celebrated Henry Pattillo agreed to supply these congregations, but only occasionally.[9]

Even though Nutbush Church and Grassy Creek are called by Downey "Twins of Old Granville Presbyterians,"[10] Nutbush acquired land for its church in 1762 and Grassy Creek in 1767. Before these two oldest Presbyterian churches in Granville County were built, the congregations of both churches met at the homes of the members.

The ancestors of John Chavis lived in the areas of Nutbush and Grassy Creek, and John Chavis himself preached at these churches when he came of age. As the history of John Chavis is related to the history of Granville County, it is also to be noted that before the coming of the Presbyterian church in Granville County, the Anglican establishment had wielded great religious power under the leadership of Samuel Benton, who had a plantation in what is now the town of Oxford. "By 1768, both of the Granville congregations had sites for their chapels."[11] In 1780, Rev. Henry Pattillo returned to form the "United Congregations of Grassy Creek and Nutbush."[12] Rev. Pattillo was born in Scotland.

The first rumblings of the American Revolution occurred in Bute County which was once a part of Lord Granville's territory. These rumblings of the regulators are found in the Nutbush Papers of the 6th of June, 1765.[13] Records of these incidents preceding the Revolutionary War are contained in the "Husbands Book about the regulation."

> This Herman Husbands came from Pennsylvania. He was a Quaker preacher who had come to North Carolina, where he held estates on the banks of the Alamance. He was a member of the lower house of the General Assembly and prominent in his community. He was a friend of Benjamin Franklin, from whom he had imbibed ideas of freedom and independence, which he preached fearlessly all over the State. He was held in great contempt by Governor Tryon.[14]

At Nutbush on June 6, 1765, Husbands made an address entitled "A Serious Address to Inhabitants of Granville County, containing a brief narrative of our deplorable situation by the wrongs we suffer." The speaker assures his audience that he was not complaining about the form of the government in the American colonies nor the laws but "the officers of the county courts and the abuses of the officers, who are sent to manage the public affairs." Husbands then gives a long list of abuses by the colonial officials, including excessive fees and robbery of cattle and land. Thus the revolutionary spirit was engendered in Nutbush in Granville County before the Mecklenburg Declaration was formed.

Even though Rev. Henry Pattillo returned for full-time pastorate of Nutbush in 1780–1801, evidence shows that he was publicly involved in Bute County in 1775. The following document of his revolutionary activities is found in the Pittman Papers concerning Bute County.[15]

NORTH CAROLINA, BUTE COUNTY

> At a meeting of the Committee for the Above County the 14 of June, 1775 at the Court House,
>
> Present, Henry Pattillo Chairman James Milner, Thomas Eaton, William Person, Green, H. W., William Tabb, Edward Jones, James Ransom, Sen., Harry Hall, William Green, Julius Nichols, Jethro Sumner & Isaac Hunter
>
> An association entered under by the Town of New Bern & County of Craven May 31, 1775 being transmitted to this comittee [sic]. We concur with them and hereby Agree and Associate under all the ties of Religion, hoping and eager ... that we will adopt and Endeavor to execute the Measures which the General Congress, now sitting at Philadelphia, may conclude on, for preserving our Constitution, and approving the Execution of the several arbitrary and Illegal acts of the *British* Parliament; and that we will readily observe the Directions of our General Committee for the purposes aforesaid, the preservation of peace and good order and Security of Individual and private property.[16]

The recommendation of the committee is that

> the good people of the County ... meet together at the Convenient places, and form themselves Independent Companies of & Chose [sic] their own officers and that the officers when Chose shall Diligently Instruct their men in Military Exercise for the Defense of this County and join in Exercises [ill.]
> The committee recommend to the People of this county ... a new Committee on the day of the General Election and also to Nominate Delegates to attend the Colony Convention at Hillsborough or whatever place shall be approved for the meeting.
>
> Signed: Henry Pattillo, Chairman
> Committee Minutes
> June 14, 1775

According to a sketch of Pattillo which accompanies his textbook *A Geographical Catechism,*

> Henry Pattillo was a man of large public spirit and took
> a deep and active interest in all matters relating to the wel-
> fare of the state and nation. He was a man, too, of great
> energy and force of character and he exerted a strong
> influence upon the political as well as the religious and
> educational life of his state. Because of his prominence, he
> was chosen one of those sent by Governor Tryon to pacify
> the Regulators.[17]

However, Rev. Pattillo was not on the side of the loyalists but
supported the regulators. He followed a tradition among the Presbyterian ministers by being a minister, a teacher, and a politician.

> He began his teaching career in Virginia while studying
> for the ministry. After coming to North Carolina he con-
> ducted schools at Hawfields, Williamsboro, and at
> Granville Hall, a school incorporated in 1779 when the
> country was convulsed in war, the exact site of which is
> not now known. He doubtless taught at several places—
> wherever, in fact, his pastoral duties called him to reside.[18]

It is very possible that John Chavis studied under Rev. Pattillo
at Granville Hall, or Williamsboro, or both. Granville Hall was a
Latin grammar school. Pattillo also taught Greek and Latin. "He is
said to have been an excellent classical scholar for his day and opportunity.... In 1787 he published in Wilmington a volume of *Sermons*;
in 1796 his *Geographical Catechism*, the first textbook written in
North Carolina, appeared."[19] He did not have elaborate textbooks,
blackboards, maps and gazetteers, so he taught his students in a
question-and-answer format. In his teaching he tried to give the student a knowledge of history, geography, and astronomy as well as a
strong belief in divine providence as the creator of all things. Instead
of having a narrow audience focus, he tried to appeal to persons from
all walks of life as well as his students. On the title page of his *Geographical Catechism,* he appealed to the reading public:

> To Read
> Newspapers, History, or Travels;
> With as Much of
> The Science of Astronomy, and the Doctrine
> of the Air,
> As is judged sufficient for the FARMER, who wishes
> to understand something of

The Works of GOD, around him;
And for the studious YOUTH, who have or have not a
prospect of
further prosecuting these SUBLIME SCIENCES

Note that Pattillo calls the physical sciences the "sublime" sciences, showing the Presbyterian view that all knowledge is a part of God's providence. The Presbyterians had a special message for the farmers (the large plantation owners), who were becoming more and more materialistic and placing religion aside. In his catechism, Pattillo writes a long panegyric of the virtues of America as a free nation:

> O my dear country! never forget your then situation. At this awful period Congress met, under a load of public cares, inconceivable by all but patriots. It seized the helm—it became a center of union and of motion, to the scattered colonists; and made a common cause with Boston. The continent, as by an electrical shock, caught the noble enthusiastic spirit of liberty and resentment.[20]

Pattillo engendered in his students a love for freedom and the exercise of their rights in all aspects of the Republic. These sentiments helped to mold the character of his students, many of whom like John Chavis became soldiers in the Revolutionary War and upholders of the rights of mankind. The seriousness of the revolutionaries is noteworthy. In forming their military units in preparation for the Revolutionary War, they advocated discipline: "Resolved by the committee that all extravagances, Dissipation & Vice particularly Cards and Racing be Discouraged and Every kind of Industry encouraged."

John never forgot about Pattillo's lecture on every man's right to life, liberty, and the pursuit of happiness. At the height of the Revolutionary War he enlisted, just as other members of the Chavis family did in Virginia and North Carolina.

A deposition of Peggy Chaves [sic] of Hertford County, North Carolina, was made on July 14, 1792, "that she is the widow of Henry Chaves DEC's ... that her husband died since the war and that her husband served nine months in the Contl Army." Later she was paid from the "account of Henry Chavers [sic] Private, with the United States for 9 mos. service from Nov. 1778–August 1779."[21]

There were many Chavises from Virginia who fought in the Revolutionary War. Several different John Chavises (with variant spellings) are listed: John Chavers of Dinwiddie; John Chavos (place unlisted); John Chaves, bounty warrant; and John Chaves, Negro of Mecklenburg County, bounty warrant. The latter refers to Rev. John Chavis. Bounty warrants were applications for grants of bounty land as a result of participation in the war. Two different Samuel Chavises are also listed.[22]

Around 1780 at the age of seventeen, John Chavis enlisted in the Fifth Virginia Regiment and served for three years in the Revolutionary War. Captain Mayo Carrington, in a bounty warrant written in March 1783, certified that Chavis had "faithfully fulfilled [his duties] and is thereby entitled to all immunities granted to three year soldiers."[23]

To defend one's property and nation from enemy attack was an act not only of patriotism but of personal honor. John Chavis had served in an honorable fashion, and when he returned to North Carolina, he needed the "bounty money" to make a headstart in taking care of his family. (He apparently did not marry, however, until 1815, when records show he married Sarah Frances Anderson.[24]) Although he applied for the bounty each year for three years, he apparently never received it. During this time he appealed to his family for assistance. In the 1789 tax list of Mecklenburg County, Virginia, "Chavis was shown as a free black whose property consisted of a single horse. In the same year he was employed by Robert Greenwood's estate as a tutor to Greenwood's orphans."[25] If he was born in 1763, he was twenty-six years old when he taught Robert Greenwood's orphans.

From the documents and circumstantial evidence, it is highly probable that John Chavis studied under Rev. Pattillo and attained sufficient knowledge to tutor Robert Greenwood's orphans in Virginia. Since his great-grandfather William Chavis held property both in Virginia and North Carolina, he could very easily have registered in the continental army in Mecklenburg County and later tutored Robert Greenwood's children. Henry Pattillo also taught in Virginia and North Carolina. All of these experiences—tutelage under the revolutionary patriot Henry Pattillo, participating in the Revolutionary War, and teaching Robert Greenwood's orphans—contributed to his educational background. By having these practical experiences, John Chavis became knowledgeable, god-fearing, and well-disciplined.

Following Chavis's study under Rev. Pattillo, his participation in the Revolutionary War, and his tutoring in Virginia, he was sent by his friends and perhaps neighbors of Abraham Plains Township, most probably the Smiths, to study at Princeton University.[26] The Trustee Minutes of Princeton University for 1778–1796 read as follows:

Nassau Hall, September 25, 1792

The Board met according to appointment. The Rev. Dr. Witherspoon, President of the Board.

Dr. John Rodgers Andrew Hunter
Dr. Robert Smith James Armstrong
Mr. Anzel Roe Jonathan B. Smith
James Boyd Isaac Snowden
John Woodhull John Beaty
Richard Stockton

Thursday morning, nine o'clock

A copy of the will of Mr. James Leslie of New York leaving a certain legacy to the Director of the Trustees of New Jersey College of the Education of poor and pious youth.

Mr. John Henry Todd of Virginia & John Chavis a free Black man of that state were recommended by the Rev'd John B. Smith to be received on this fund.[27]

The Rev. John Blair Smith and Rev. Henry Pattillo were closely acquainted, not only as ministers but as a business partners.[28] The above document verifies that John Chavis's admission to Princeton University was approved by the trustees. Tradition maintains that he studied at Princeton University from 1792 to 1795. These were enough years to finish his academic degree, but his name is not listed with the graduates. At Princeton, he studied as a private student under President John Witherspoon at his home called Tusculum, just outside of the city of Princeton. Many writers attest to the fact that Chavis attended Princeton: Smith,[29] Johnson,[30] Bassett,[31] Weeks,[32] Boyd,[33] Knight,[34] Shaw,[35]; and Woodson.[36]

Tradition also says that John Chavis was sent to Princeton as a wager among his white neighbors who sent him there to "see if a Negro would take a collegiate education." Bassett was one of the first writers to refer to this assertion. Even though this statement has been historically attractive (as evidenced by its being repeated constantly), it may not be the whole truth. The reason that he was sent to Princeton was not that simplistic. Other black students had attended Princeton before John Chavis arrived. According to Knight, "One or two Negro students and several Delaware Indians were there under Witherspoon."[37] Chavis had already shown much

Top: Engraving of Tusculum, home of Princeton president John Witherspoon, as it looked in the 1790s. (Princeton University Libraries.) *Bottom:*
Photograph of Tusculum today.

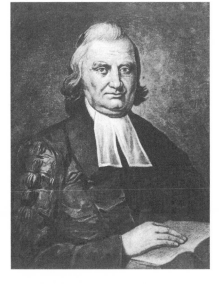

promise after having attended Rev. Pattillo's school and also enough education to have tutored Robert Greenwood's orphans in 1789. Therefore, first of all he was not sent to Princeton just because he was a Negro, but because he showed academic promise. Secondly, the Presbyterians wanted their ministers to be highly educated, and they envisioned Chavis as a future minister who would preach the gospel, especially to the slaves. (See the next chapter on his preaching ministry.)

Furthermore, the curriculum at Princeton was based upon a prior

Top: The Barn at Tusculum. *Bottom:* John Witherspoon (1723–1794), sixth president of Princeton University, statesman, scholar, clergyman, and signer of the Declaration of Independance. Witherspoon taught John Chavis in Witherspoon's home. (Daguerrotype from *President Witherspoon: A Biography* by Varnum Collins, published in 1928 by Princeton University Press. Reprinted by permission of Princeton University Press.)

Picture of Washington College as it looked in 1802, landscape view. (The Library of Virginia.)

education at a Latin grammar school such as Rev. Pattillo operated. The students entering were tested upon the following:

> English, including English Grammar, Orthography, Punctuation, Short and Simple English Composition; Geography, ancient and Modern, and United States History. Latin consisted of Latin Grammar (including Prosody), Caesar (five books of the Commentaries), Sallust (Catiline or Jugurtha), Virgil (six books of Aeneid), Cicero's Select orations (six), Arnold's Latin Prose Composition (twelve chapters). Greek consisted of Greek Grammar (including Prosody), Goodwin's Greek Reader (111 pages), or Xenophon (three books of the Anabasis), Homer (the first two books of the Iliad, except the Catalogue of the Ships), and Arnold's Greek Prose (thirty exercises with special reference to writing with the accents); and Mathematics which consisted of Arithmetic (including the Metric system), Algebra (on through Quadratic Equations of one unknown quantity) and Geometry (first book of Euclid).[38]

As president-teacher at Princeton University, John Witherspoon prepared the way for curriculum development. He introduced the

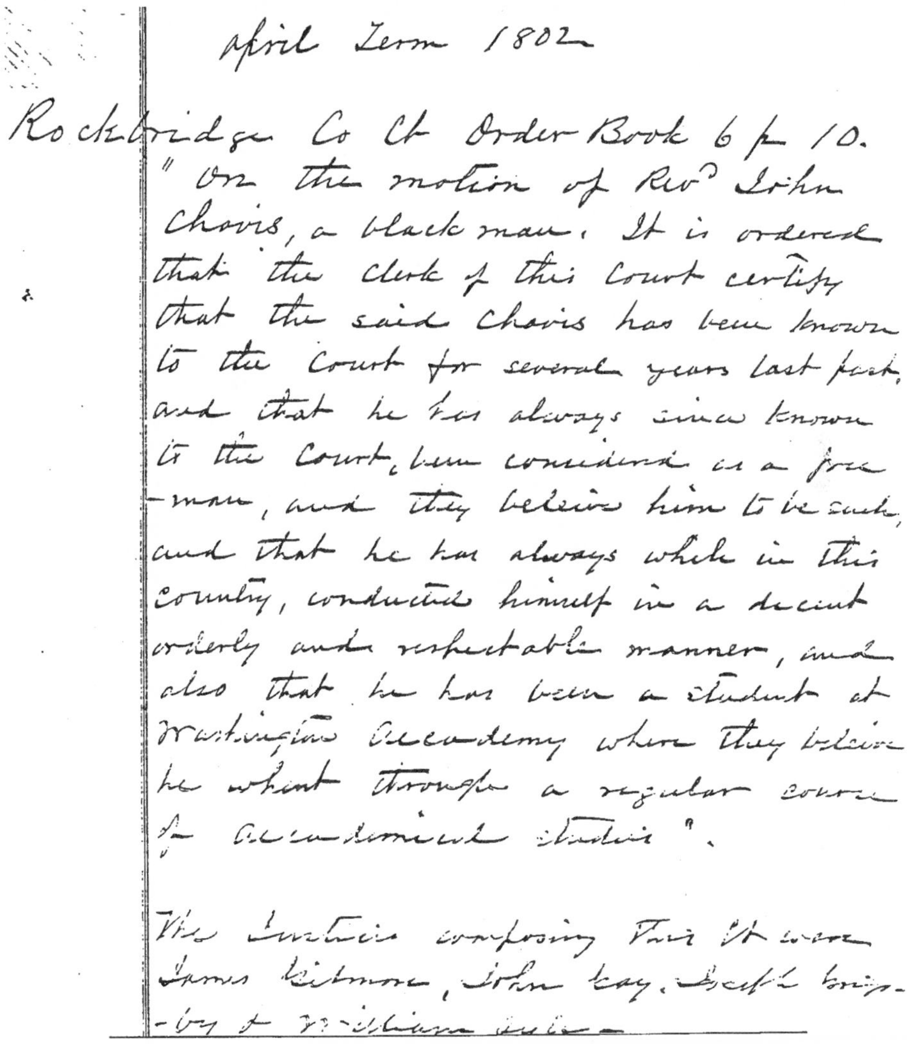

[Handwritten document:]

April Term 1802

Rockbridge Co Ct Order Book 6 p 10.
" On the motion of Revd John
Chavis, a black man. It is ordered
that the Clerk of this Court certify
that the said Chavis has been known
to the Court for several years last past,
and that he has always since known
to the Court, been considered as a free
man, and they believe him to be such,
and that he has always while in this
county, conducted himself in a decent
orderly and respectable manner, and
also that he has been a student at
Washington Academy where they believe
he went through a regular course
of academical studies ".

The Justices composing this Ct were
James Kitmore, John Kay, Joseph Smith-
by & William ____

This document makes reference to John Chavis's completion of his studies at Washington College in 1802. Rockbridge County, Virginia Order Book 1802–1802, page 10 (Reel 36). (Archives Research Services, The Library of Virginia, Richmond, VA.)

physical sciences, as well as the mental sciences, in addition to the study of modern languages, such as English, French and German.[39]

Practically all of the Presbyterian ministers of the eighteenth century had studied at Princeton. Rev. Pattillo had studied there before Witherspoon's time but had not graduated. Witherspoon, like Pattillo, was very active in the revolutionary cause. Before and during the Revolutionary War, he was an absentee president, attending the various continental congresses. According to Varnum Collins, secretary of Princeton University and biographer of Witherspoon, the British spies pinpointed Witherspoon as an anti–British revolutionary: "Wentworth had already named him to William Ede as a leader on the anti–British side, and Lord Carlisle's list of American leaders in June 1778, similarly includes him."[40]

As a teacher, Witherspoon taught moderation and common sense in all things. "The clergyman should not despise the intellectuals," he wrote; "neither should the intellectuals be too proud to call themselves Christians." Even though regular prayer service was held as well as religious discussions about literature, Witherspoon fostered a nonsectarian atmosphere on the campus.[41] He believed in and practiced academic freedom. Not only did the students study about religion, but they also learned the views of philosophers such as Voltaire, Volney, and Thomas Paine. Another tradition of Princeton was to uphold the mental and moral sciences which were being neglected by the promotion of materialism.[42]

The common-sense views and critical reasoning about literature and moral philosophy were taught by Dr. Witherspoon. He also preached the "doctrine that education and religious freedom went hand in hand with civil liberty."[43]

Graduates of Princeton became founders of colleges and leaders in the Presbyterian Church:

> Over eleven per cent of them became Presidents of colleges in eight different States of the Union. Princetonians of his breeding were first Presidents of Union College, New York; Washington College and Hampden-Sidney College in Virginia; Mount Zion College in South Carolina; Queen's College and the University of North Carolina in that State, and of Washington, Greenville, Tusculum and Cumberland Colleges and the University of Nashville in Tennessee.[44]

Following in the footsteps of his predecessors, John Chavis continued his studies at Washington College (now known as Washington and Lee University). After leaving Princeton around 1793 or 1794, he completed his "academical" studies at Washington College in 1802. Documentation of his presence at Washington College is found in the Rockbridge County Court Order Book Number 6.[45]

Thus, John Chavis received a rich classical as well as modern education for his time. This education, stressing religious freedom, excellence, service to mankind, and liberty, would imbue him with the knowledge and wisdom needed in his teaching and ministerial professions.

CHAPTER 3

Chavis's Christian Ministry

> I rode on, one of the most miserable of men, and found
> no peace of mind until I became satisfactorily convinced
> that the atonement which our Saviour had made was com-
> mensurate to the spiritual wants of the WHOLE HUMAN FAM-
> ILY: that he had made it possible for each individual to be
> saved.... I have had the doctrine of the Atonement of
> Christ, of God's decrees and of election, under investiga-
> tion for about forty years. And although upon those sub-
> jects, I have read the writings of some of the greatest men
> the world had produced, yet they left those doctrines
> wrapped up in so much mystery that I could not be
> satisfied with their investigation.[1]

To understand the call of John Chavis to the Christian ministry,
one must visualize the urgency to convert Africans and Indians during the colonial period. The American quest for freedom during the
pre–Revolutionary period and the concomitant participation in the
institution of slavery are two of the persistent ironies of American
history. The following estimation is given by Jernigan:

> Before the Revolution probably a million negroes had
> lived as slaves within the boundaries of the American
> colonies But, in spite of the fact that religious motives were
> so prominent in the settlement of these colonies, and reli-
> gion was a subject which occupied the thought and effort
> of private individuals, denominations, missionary societies,
> and even legislative bodies to an extraordinary degree,
> most of the slaves lived and died strangers to Christianity.[2]

At the beginning of the slave trade in the seventeenth century
among Englishmen, the Church of England and the Society for the
Propagation of the Gospel in Foreign Parts were active in advocating

conversion. There were many obstacles to the conversion of the slaves. For one thing, pro-slavery apologists claimed that "heathens and barbarians" because of their infidelity were "doomed to eternal perdition." Furthermore, slave owners feared that conversion and baptism of the slaves would lead to their freedom.[3] Attempting to resolve the conflict between religious conversion and slavery, the slavery apologists took an ambivalent stand. "While positively denying that conversion or baptism was sufficient reason for enfranchisement and insisting that all slaves must serve for life," Jernigan writes, "they at the same time called upon masters to use their efforts to convert slaves to the Christian religion."[4]

In order to prevent the possible loss of property (the slaves) but encourage the promulgation the Christian religion, laws were enacted on this issue of conversion. Jernigan tells us that "Between 1664 and 1706 at least six of the colonies passed acts" addressing the perceived problem. "Maryland (1664) declared that all slaves must serve for life in order to prevent damage which masters might sustain if their slaves pretended to be Christians and so pleaded the law of England."[5]

Virginia followed Maryland with the act of 1667 which declared "that slaves by birth were not freed when baptized." This act allegedly was designed so "that diverse masters, ffreed [sic] from this doubt, may more carefully endeavor that propagation of Christianity by permitting children, though slaves or those of greater growth if capable to be admitted to that sacrament."[6]

A Virginia act of 1670 stated that only those imported by shipping and not already Christians were to be slaves for life. This act was repealed, however, because it did not discriminate against the Christian slave in favor of the "English or other Christian."[7] Through the passage of laws, virtually all slaves, Christian or not, were confined to slavery for a lifetime. By the eighteenth century, there was great activity during the Age of Enlightenment to foster conversion among the slaves in the American colonies. "The Society for Promoting Christian Learning sent books, catechisms, etc. (1755–1761) to Samuel Davies of Virginia, for distribution among the negroes."[8] According to Jernigan, the Christian authorities were as ambivalent as the legal authorities toward the conversion of slaves.

> The Church of England did not raise the question of the right of its members to hold slaves, denied that there was any inconsistency between Christianity and slavery, and

made no effort to emancipate negroes because of religious
scruples. Indeed the Bishop of London had declared, in
1727, that Christianity did not make "the least Alteration
in Civil Property; that the Freedom which Christianity
gives, is a Freedom from the Bondage of Sin and Satan, and
from the Dominion of those Lusts and Passions and inordi-
nate Desires, but as to their outward condition they
remained as before even after baptism."[9]

Not only the clergy of the Church of England but the clergy of
the Protestant sects, including the Presbyterians, owned slaves.
According to Jernigan, "the Friends alone, before the Revolution,
seriously questioned, because of religious scruples, the right of church
members to hold slaves. The Society of Friends was the only denomination that gradually forced members who held slaves to dispose of
them or suffer expulsion from the church."[10] One can verify this by
studying the tax records and inventories of estates of clergymen of
all denominations during the seventeenth through the first half of
the nineteenth Century.

As the institution of slavery became more profitable and larger
numbers of slaves were imported, the planters and slavocracy became
more prejudiced about the conversion of these newly imported
Africans:

"Guinea" negroes as they were often called, could not be
converted successfully. A sharp distinction was drawn,
however, between this class and those born in the colonies.
Not only were the former stupid, but adult imported
negroes failed to learn the English language well enough to
appreciate or profit by religious instruction, a fact fre-
quently commented on by the clergy. On the other hand,
those born in the country were considered more intelligent,
and generally could learn English well enough for such purposes.[11]

Thus the clergy among the slavemasters set up a type of class
system, distinguishing between the newly imported Africans and the
"naturalized" slaves. They used religious dogma to justify the lack
of conversion of the slaves, but their reasons were purely political
and economic.

Some progress is seen in the conversion of slaves from 1724 to
1776 in Virginia through the work of the Presbyterians. Jernigan

points to letters written by Presbyterian ministers in the colony from 1750 to 1761. For example, a 1750 letter by Samuel Davies "reports that there were as many as a thousand negroes in Virginia converted and baptized, about one hundred belonging to Presbyterians."[12]

The movement toward conversion of slaves spread to South Carolina with Rev. Mr. Harrison (1759) of St. James (Goose Creek) parish and Rev. Mr. Clark of St. Phillip's in Charleston (1757–1758). Clark complained that there "was great negligence among white people respecting the religious education of negroes and laments that there was not a 'Civil Establishment' in the Colony for the Christian Instruction of fifty thousand negro Slaves."[13]

Although there were not many slaves in the Middle Colonies and in New England, there was still resistance against conversion, as reported by the Society for the Propagation of the Gospel:

> Although there were about 1400 negroes and Indian slaves in New York City (1725/6), the catechist of the S.P.G. writes that from 1732–1740 but 219 had been baptized, only twenty-four of whom were adults.[14]

In the southern states where there were the greatest numbers of slaves there was the greatest resistance against conversion for fear that the slave would become more intelligent through religious instruction or be subject to manumission.

From such a wasteland of oppression, the Presbyterians developed fertile vineyards for their work. Their first mission was to carry the Gospel to the Indians in the South during the colonial period. Although "Moravians sent missionaries to the Cherokees in North Carolina, and Wesleyans attempted work among the same tribe in Georgia ... little or nothing was accomplished."[15] The first Presbyterian missionary sent by the Society for the Propagation of the Gospel was John Martin, whose studies had been directed by Samuel Davies and who was to serve as the first candidate of Hanover Presbytery according to their order of June 7, 1758. However, a concerted effort to convert and educate the Indians did not occur until after the Revolutionary War. Presbyterian Gideon Blackburn is generally credited as the first of his denomination to succeed in converting Indians in the South. Beginning his missionary work in 1804, Blackburn learned to work with the Indians and to hold council in mutual respect with them. He established schools among the Cherokee. The Cherokee thus became well versed in the study of religion and advanced learning. Failing health forced Blackburn's departure from the Cherokee Missions in 1870, but he was succeeded by "Cyrus Kingsbury who set up his first station among the Cherokees, called Brainerd, near Chattanooga (now known as Missionary Ridge)."[16] As a result of accepting the Christian religion and its concomitant education, various Indian tribes began adopting and accepting the ways and customs of the white man. Among them were the Cherokees, Chickasaws, Choctaws, Creeks, and Osages.[17]

The Presbyterians were interested in the conversion of not only the Indians but also the Negroes in the South. Rev. Henry Pattillo, pastor of Grassy Creek and Nutbush churches in Granville County, North Carolina, administered to mixed congregations of whites and blacks. John Chavis, a budding scholar and catechist of Pattillo, often preached in Pattillo's churches. Pattillo was one of the persons who encouraged Chavis to attend Princeton University. As seen in the previous chapter, Pattillo was also closely associated with Rev. John Blair Smith, the trustee of Princeton University, who submitted Chavis's name as a candidate for admission to the university under the Leslie Fund.

Therefore after John Chavis had finished Princeton and studied for the ministry at Washington College in Virginia, he was picked by the Presbyterian Church as a fit candidate. Samuel Davies, a prominent minister of the period, confessed that there was a movement among Presbyterians, especially in Virginia, to convert thousands of blacks between 1750 and 1761. On October 19, 1799, the Lexington Presbytery of Virginia met at Lexington and discussed the application John had made to become a minister of the gospel.[18] He was allowed to go through the examining process. The minutes acknowledged that "notwithstanding his color" the Presbytery agreed "to take him under their care for further trials in the usual form." By the next meeting he was supposed to give an exegesis (an explanation) in Latin on the theme "in quo consistat salvatio ab peccato" (What is necessary for salvation from sin?) and a homily (a sermon) on the decree of Election.

John had heard as early as June 1800 that the Presbytery was considering his application. His heart must have beat as fast as blacksmith's bellow when he received word about the Presbytery's decision and he began preparing for the "trial."

One problem he faced was that his eyesight was beginning to fail. On June 11, 1800, he was supposed to attend a meeting at Tinkling Spring Meeting House in Virginia but could not because of his eyesight. Although he was only thirty-seven years old in 1800, he also suffered from rheumatism which remained with him through old age. In spite of his infirmities, however, at the meeting which began at Louisburg on Thursday, October 23, 1800,[19] and ended on Saturday, October 25, 1800, he gave a successful exegesis and homily on the topics that had been assigned him at the previous meeting.

At the meeting on Saturday, October 25th, a Rev. Mr. Wilson informed the Presbytery, "I wish balances due me for expenses to the General Assembly be appropriated to the use of John Chavis provided the said Chavis shall be licensed to preach the Gospel." After Mr. Wilson agreed to help John financially, the chairman of the assembly told the clerk of the presbytery, "Ascertain the amount of said balance and give Mr. Chevis [another misspelling] an order on the Treasurer for whatever may appear to be due the Rev. Mr. Wilson." The chairman of the Presbytery then asked John to lecture on Psalm 23. His lecture must have met or even exceeded their expectations, for at the end of that session, the chairman announced that John had completed that part of his trial satisfactorily.

At another meeting at Timber Ridge Meeting House on Tuesday evening, November 18, 1800, the chairman asked that John take another trial examination on the languages of sciences. John apologetically replied that because of the weakness of his eyes, he could not do so at that time.[20] Then one of the elders who was against the prolongation of John Chavis's trials arose and suggested,

> Mr. Chavis being a man of colour, and as there is a prospect of his being peculiarly useful to those of his own complexion, the Presbytery supposes his case something extraordinary and therefore agrees to dispense with these parts of trial, and proceed to his examination on deviltry.[21]

At that point a questioner or interlocutor from the elders began asking John questions about deviltry. Through his answers John apparently showed that he had read widely from the Presbyterian theological books on the subject. It is probable that he traced the origin of deviltry to the rebellion of Satan and the subsequent original sin committed by Adam and Eve, giving the practical implications of the biblical story of man's perverted will. The legend that this black man could speak with polish and poise must have been realized as he spoke on the subject of original sin, a subject which was sacrosanct to the clergy of that period. The elders then voted unanimously to sustain John's examination "as a satisfactory part of trial."

On the next day John preached a sermon from Acts 16, verse 9: "Believe on the Lord Jesus Christ and thou shalt be saved." When he finished, they asked him questions about his sermon, possibly testing his theological learnings on topics such as preordination and the salvation of the unelected. These topics have long created opposing camps within the church. Clearly John answered well. At the end of the interrogation, the elders announced that because of John's satisfactory presentation, they had agreed to grant him the license to preach.[22]

John's heart must have leaped like the sun on Easter morning. He would be the first black person in America to be ordained by the Presbyterian Church! Then the elders, eager to establish the parameters of this revolutionary act, explained to Rev. Chavis that he was given latitude to travel within and without the bounds of Lexington Presbytery, but he had a special mission to preach to the black race. Since they wanted to convert more of the blacks who were held in the captivity of slavery, they believed that Rev. Chavis could do the job better than a white minister.

However, Rev. Chavis preached to more white people than blacks. (See Chavis's reports to the Presbytery below.)[23] He continued to preach at the meetings of the Presbytery, traveling back and forth on horseback there and to different congregations.

Rev. Henry Pattillo still kept an eye on his protégé. After Chavis had preached at the Rocky Spring Meeting House on Tuesday, June 9, 1801, from Malachi 4, verses 1 and 2, "Behold the day cometh that shall burn as an oven...," he brought forth a letter which had been written by Rev. Pattillo, addressed to the Elders of Lexington Presbytery:

> I do herein request that Rev. John Chavis who has preached under my inspection for many years be dismissed from Lexington Presbytery in order to be put under the care of the Presbytery of Hanover.[24]

The Presbytery of Hanover was the same presbytery with which Pattillo was affiliated. After speculation upon the request, the leader of the elders declared, "Mr. Chevis [sic] is hereby dismissed from this Presbytery and is recommended to the care of the Presbytery of Hanover as a man of exemplary piety and possessed of many qualifications which merit their respectful attention."[25]

Excerpt from Minutes of the Standing
Committee of Missions May 21, 1803

Mr. John Chavis introduces his narrative by reminding
the Assembly, that at the time of making his former report
three months of the time for which he had been engaged
were unexpired; he has since completed that tour of duty
by visiting as a missionary the western parts of Virginia,
which appear to present natural obstacles that require no
small share of zeal and perseverance to surmount them. He
met with very friendly receptions and great kindness from
the people in those parts, who seem to have attended the
preaching of the word in as great numbers as could reason-
ably have been expected—to have heard it gladly, and in
some instances profitably.

The following statement is made by the Committee from
Mr. Chavis's Journal, to give the Assembly a view of the
number and proportion of *blacks* who attended Divine Service,

	Whites	*Blacks*
In Bedford County about	150 persons attended	no blacks are mentioned
Rock Bridge Ditto	100	Ditto
Lexington Ditto	400	100, a revival of religion here.
Falling Spring	50	none mentioned
Kanawah	200	30
Ditto meeting house	30	
Kanford's	30	none
Morris's	30	

(mentions an old African woman as being much affected and weeping.)

	Whites	*Blacks*
Johnson's	50	none mentioned
Kanawah Court House	150	50
George Lee's	100	none mentioned

(a revival of religion among the Baptists.)

	Whites	*Blacks*
Kanawah River about	80 persons attended	no blacks are mentioned
Ditto	60	Ditto
Coal River	200	20

(here one opposer for religion was made to fall and weep.
He never saw a people more desirous to be instructed.)

	Whites	*Blacks*
Kanawah Courthouse	100	15
E. Hughes's	180	5
(Baptist meeting house in Green Briar County)	200	20

(numbers appeared to be deeply imprest; he was strongly solicited to settle here.)

Lewisburgh	250	50
Bototourt County	200	50
Rockbridge Ditto-Lebanon	200	80

(In the tour he preached 23 sermons, and received $7.74.)

He began his mission under the appointment of last year, on the 18th of July, and continued in it for 7 months and 3 weeks, traveling in the Counties in Mecklenburg, Lunenburg, and Nottoway in Virginia; and in Granville, Person, Wake, Warren, Orange, Chatham, Randolph, and Caswell, in North Carolina. In this tour he preached 68 times, and delivered 8 exhortations; attended several religious societies, assisted twice in the administration of the Lord's Supper, and collected $1.86. He was several times prevented from preaching, by bodily indisposition.

The proportion of Blacks who attended was greater than on his former route, as appears from the following statement of the numbers of his congregation on different occasions, Visit,

Mecklinburg	persons 250	Blacks 50
Person	500	150
Ditto	35	15
Ditto	40	15
Mecklinburg	800	300
Lunenburg	150	
Mecklinburg	persons 50	Blacks
Bluestone	200	50
Ditto	150	50
New Bethel	300	100
Person	200	10
Wake	600	50
Person	250	80
Warren	30	20
Granville	250	10
Gillarns Meeting House	300	80
Granville	150	30
Chatham	450	150
Ditto	300	50
Ditto	70	20
Ditto	400	150
Granville	30	10
Caswell	200	20
Granville	400	150
Cullon's, a Baptist Meeting House	150	50
Poplar Creek	250	80
Granville	500	180

In Mr. Chavis's Journal are some passages which the
Committee deem worthy of being particularly communi-
cated, and they think it proper on this occasion to use Mr.
Chavis's own words. [Here Mr. Chavis's report for
1801–1802 was read.] The reports of the missionaries
excited mixed emotions in the minds of your Committee—
they are pleased with the diligence and fidelity, and with
the success, on many instances, of those heralds of the
Cross:—they read with delight, of whitening fields which
promise an abundant harvest; but it is a painful reflection
that much of it appears to be in danger of being lost for
want of laborers; wherever they look, they find a scarcity
of these—few offer themselves for the work, although he
that laboureth receiveth wages and gathereth fruit unto life
eternal;—and Presbyteries, unable to assist your Committee,
call upon them for aid;—Shall they then despair? No! The
Lord of the Harvest will, in his own time, send labourers
into it: "The wilderness, and the solitary place, shall yet be
glad, and the desert shall rejoice, and blossom as the rose.
It shall blossom abundantly, and rejoice even with joy and
singing:—the glory of Lebanon shall be given to it, the
excellency of Carmel and Sharon:—they shall see the glory
of the Lord, and the excellency of our God!"[26]

John must have felt a sense of ease at being allowed to move to
a more familiar territory, for he had been a riding missionary for the
Presbytery of Hanover under Rev. Pattillo's leadership. He was the
first black home missionary in the Presbyterian Church. According
to reliable reports, his sermons were eloquent and universally appealing. He had wanted to preach more to "his own people," but there
were very few churches that would allow the slaves to enter. Very
often he would preach to the slaves under a grove of trees, or in an
open field when the sun was not scorching hot.

The slaves learned about the biblical stories by listening to such
ministers as Rev. Chavis. They made up songs based upon the biblical stories, which later became known as spirituals. Such spirituals as "Joshua Fit the battle of Jericho," "Go Down Moses," and
"Didn't It Rain, Chillun" came out of the slaves' understanding of
the Christian sermons and their experiences with hardship and toil.
The singing of the slaves and the creation of their soulful rhythms
were sermons in song, an extension of the sermons that they heard.
Perhaps Rev. Chavis was deeply moved by the singing of fellow
blacks who were bound to involuntary servitude and wondered

about the ironies of preaching spiritual devotion even as the cruel institution of slavery continued.

Committed people during those days seem to have had great physical as well as spiritual stamina. Rev. Chavis went on horseback from state to state, to Maryland, Virginia, South Carolina, and North Carolina, through 1807. Finally he decided that he would leave the Presbytery of Hanover; in 1814 he joined the Orange Presbytery, where he remained a minister until 1834.[27] He then joined the Roanoke Presbytery, where he continued his membership until his death in 1838. Among the churches where he preached to whites and blacks in his home county of Granville were Shiloh, Nutbush, and Island Creek.

The tranquillity of the early 1800s did not last long because in spite of the Great Revolution that was fought for the freedom of the colonists, slavery persisted. It reached its zenith near the middle of the 1800s. More slaves were being imported. Because of the harsh and inhuman treatment of the slaves, such as severe beatings, torture, rape, mutilations of runaways, sexual abuse, starvation and other forms of animalistic tactics employed by slave masters, rebellion and discontent festered on the plantations. In the slave holders' attempts to dehumanize the newly imported slaves and to create a sense of inferiority among them in contrast to the treatment of the house servants, slaves began meeting clandestinely in deep groves during the darkness of the night, in cabins where they huddled together over tin tubs filled with water to keep the sound from escaping or in thick cornfields where the tassels of yellow corn kept their deep secrets. Those servants who had access to the Big House and who secretly learned to read became preachers. But the sermons which they preached to their fellow slaves and the songs which the slaves in turn sang became sermons and songs of rebellion.

Just a few miles from the North Carolina eastern border and in some of the same places where Rev. Chavis had preached, there arose Nat Turner, a self-proclaimed preacher, with a vision of the Black Moses or Messiah who would lead his people out of the degradation of slavery. His followers were few at first, but the numbers grew as they believed in his vision. The plan was methodically put into motion. He talked to his troops about how they would attack and destroy the slave masters and the institutions of slavery, and how God had called him to lead his people to freedom. After freedom, they would march triumphantly into Jerusalem. Jerusalem was the name of the county seat in the county of Southampton in Virginia,

Nat's home. So empowered were his followers with the fervor of the dream of freedom, that they could not see the possible repercussions of their acts. So on a Sunday morning in 1831, Nat and his converts went from mansion to mansion murdering men, women, and children. They did not spare anyone in their path.

This was not the first time that blacks had expressed open rebellion against slavery. Denmark Veasey had attempted an insurrection in Charleston, South Carolina, and had failed because some of the slaves had revealed the plans to the masters. Gabriel Prosser in Virginia was another slave warrior. Also there had been a white minister from out of the state before the Nat Turner rebellion who had circulated a letter of rebellion in Orange County in North Carolina. The letter was David Walker's Appeal to the Slaves. A letter from Joseph Hinton to John Gray Blount expresses the uneasiness of the slave masters about the prospect of rebellion. Rev. Chavis, who became spokesman for his race, was asked by some of the slave holders in Orange County (where the Orange Presbytery was located) about the letter and the fact that it preached open rebellion. He fearlessly replied, "I am not surprised. It is very possible that violence could erupt under the present dangerous circumstances."[28]

Later, after the Nat Turner rebellion, Rev. Chavis wrote to Congressman Willie P. Mangum, who had been one of his students and for whom he had been a lifetime mentor, about the cruelties of American justice toward black people. (Congressman Mangum later became a United States senator.) A white congressman from North Carolina had castrated a black man for allegedly having had sexual intercourse with the congressman's wife. Chavis told Mangum he didn't believe either the castrated man or Nat Turner was guilty of the crimes they were accused of.[29] He said that the murders, the castration, and the hanging of Nat Turner were abominable crimes. He believed that there was an inherent wrong in the criminal justice system and in legal proceedings against black people.

Rev. Chavis did not know that soon his own life would be entrapped in these proceedings, for the planters felt that their whole word would fall apart in the wake of Nat Turner's rebellion. Many southern states, including North Carolina, enacted laws forbidding blacks from preaching and teaching. In 1832 the North Carolina legislature passed an Act for the better regulation of the conduct of negroes, slaves and free persons of color." According to Edgar Knight, a journalist and historian:

The Statute made it unlawful for any free Negro, slave,
or free person of color to preach or exhort in public (under
any pretense) or in any manner to officiate as a preacher or
teacher in any prayer meeting or other association for worship where slaves of different families were collected
together; any free Negro or free person of color who was
duly convicted or indicted before any court having jurisdiction thereof was for each offense to receive not exceeding
thirty-nine lashes on his bare back.[30]

Rev. Chavis apparently knew all too well his predicament then,
what he really felt all the while. While he was legally free, he was
not politically free, for he could be turned into a slave just like his
brothers and sisters with the push of a pen. The law seemed to be
created just for him. In his homespun manner, he probably remem-
bered the warnings he had given his white associates about the dan-
gers of slavery and pondered how he would be able to survive the
new, unjust laws.

Perhaps deep in the recesses of his mind was a beam of hope
that he would be spared the injustice of having his sole sources of
livelihood taken away, because of his close association with certain
officials of the state such as his friend Willie P. Mangum and state
treasurer Haywood. Possibly he would be allowed to continue on
the grounds that his free black students would otherwise be deprived
of an education, and free blacks and slaves would not be able to hear
the word of God. Also he had been a teacher and revered preacher
to white congregations across piedmont North Carolina. He apparently reached down into his inner reserves and attempted to ignore
the verdict, for he continued to pursue the acquisition of property
and to build a home which he could leave for his family.

As a result of the restrictions which denied him the right to
preach and teach, Rev. John Chavis could hardly afford to keep up
the small house which he had been forced to move into and to feed
his wife and children. He appealed to the Orange Presbytery for
relief, but they condescended to the court's decision, invoking God's
providence. A record of the Orange Presbytery dated April 21, 1832,
at Raleigh during the 124th Session reads:

A letter was received from Mr. John Chavis, free man of
color, and a licentiate under the care of the Presbytery, stating his difficulties and embarrassments in consequence of
an act passed at the last Session of the Legislature of this
State, forbidding free people of color to preach.

Whereupon,
Resolved, that Presbytery in view of all the circumstances
of the case recommend to their licentiate to acquiesce in
the decision of the Legislature referred to until God in his
providence shall open to him the path of duty, in regard to
the exercise of his ministry.[31]

Rev. Chavis continued to appeal to the Orange Presbytery for
help. They answered by taking up a collection for him amounting
to $52.42. In addition they would remove him from preaching and
make him a member of some Presbyterian church.

Being unable to support himself on the meager donations and
eager to express God's words, he thought of the idea of publishing
a sermonical essay on the Atonement. The subject of the Atonement
was at the heart of a controversy in the Presbyterian Church. Ministers and theologians had written on the subject before, but Rev.
Chavis had fresh ideas about an old subject. He had appealed to the
Presbytery at New Hope for help in publishing his essay. They replied
on September 4, 1833, that they were forwarding the request to members of the Presbytery for consideration and that the "same committee would take care of all matters pertaining to Mr. Chavis's
case." The essay was committed to Dr. McPheeters, Dr. Graham,
and Mr. Read to assess. The next day at the same meeting, the committee that was appointed to consider Rev. Chavis's request ruled
that they could do nothing toward the publication of his *Letter Upon
the Doctrine of the Extent of the Atonement of Christ* because it
"would not be generally interesting, and the proceeds would probably constitute nothing towards his support."[32]

The report from this meeting provides ample evidence of the
committee's condescending attitude toward John Chavis. For example, the white ministers called each other "Dr." but refused to refer
to him as "Reverend"—he was "Mr. Chavis" throughout." There is
also the fact that even among ministers, everything had to be prefaced by race. He was not just a man—a freeborn American man and
revolutionary soldier—but to them he was "a man of color" whose
boundaries they were privileged to determine.

Chavis apparently felt betrayed by the committee's rejection of
the work he had carefully and astutely researched. He perhaps
thought about the injustices of being treated as a second class citi-
zen although being free and well-educated, as well as being denied
the fulfillment of having his thoughts published. Perhaps he won-

dered how three men no older or wiser than himself could dictate how he should support himself. Whatever his feelings, this fiery, determined black man, went ahead and published *Letter Upon the Doctrine of the Extent of the Atonement of Christ* through J. Gales and Son publishing company in Raleigh, North Carolina, in 1837.

By this time he had left the Orange Presbytery and had become a Licentiate of Roanoke Presbytery, which he joined in 1836 and where he remained until 1838, the year he died.

On close examination of his *Atonement,* one sees how John Chavis's words opposed the church elders' beliefs. The sermon highlights the controversy between the Old School and the New School— the long-held doctrine of each person's predestination for heaven or hell, versus a more encompassing vision of grace available to all through free choice. Chavis's *Atonement,* though carefully framed in classical, scholarly terms, was a passionate argument against a doctrine that the old school was fighting to maintain. It is not too much to imagine that the committee reviewing *The Atonement* found it frightening, and hurried to construct reasons against its publication. Fortunately, Chavis was unwilling to let the matter rest, and he achieved his goal as he always did—through determination, perseverance, and faith.

An introduction and the full text of Letter Upon the Doctrine of the Extent of the Atonement of Christ *are found in Part II of this study.*

CHAPTER 4

A Trailblazer in the Teaching Profession

"They will not be taught [properly] unless they are taught by me."[1]

John Chavis came a long way from a free indentured servant of James Milner of Halifax County, North Carolina, in 1773 to an excellent scholar, revolutionary soldier, brilliant preacher, and respected teacher of the sons and daughters of prominent white families as well as free children of color. The earliest record of his teaching career is found in Mecklenburg County, Virginia, in 1789 where, according to Barbara Parramore, "he was employed by Robert Greenwood's estate as a tutor to Greenwood's orphans."[2] In order to become a tutor, he had to be well educated.

As indicated in Chapter 2, it is very probable that Chavis had attended school under Rev. Henry Pattillo at either Granville Hall or Williamsboro, because Pattillo not only preached to whites and blacks in the same congregation but also taught white and black children in his classical school[3] at Hawfields, Williamsboro, and at Granville Hall. If Chavis was Milner's indentured servant, he had likely been prepared as a child through reading for classical training. As a child working for Milner he was surrounded by a vast library of books on almost every imaginable subject.

John Chavis was further prepared to teach by attending Princeton University from around 1792 to 1794, followed by his attending Washington College in Rockbridge County, Virginia (later to be called Washington and Lee University). He received his certificate in 1802 for completion of his studies there. His classical education and Presbyterian ministerial career prepared him to teach his students not only the liberal arts but also religious ideals and moral philosophy.

One of the earliest records of John Chavis's teaching in his classical school is the study by Charles Lee Smith.[4] Smith refers to him

An unknown artist's illustration of John Chavis conducting classes for both white and black students. (North Carolina Division of Archives and History, Raleigh.)

as "a Presbyterian clergyman and an eminent teacher." Smith also acknowledges his debt to Rev Charles Phillips, D.D., L.L.D., of the University of North Carolina, who undertook in 1883 to collect data pertaining to John Chavis (cited in Chapters 1 and 2). Professor Smith suggests that Chavis left Princeton to become a minister in Virginia at the request of the Rev. Samuel Davies and that Rev. Henry Pattillo urged him to return to North Carolina about 1805.[5] It was apparently around 1805 that Chavis opened a classical school in Raleigh, where he taught white and black children.

Mrs. Inez Brooks of Raleigh recalls that there was a Chavis School located on South Street where the present North Carolina Association of Educators' building is now located. Mrs. Brooks, who is in her nineties, says that when she was in grade school, her teacher, Ms. Rachel McCauley, would take her and a group of children to Chavis School.[6] However, this school, which closed in the 1930s was perhaps simply named after John Chavis.

John Chavis's classical school was at first integrated, but later it was segregated because of the urging of white parents.[7] Because of the mounting intolerance of the white parents against his integrated school, Chavis was forced to place the following ad in the *Raleigh Register.*

JOHN CHAVES takes this method of informing his Employers, and the Citizens of Raleigh in general, that the present Quarter of his School will end the 15th of September, and the next will commence on the 19th. He will, at the same, time, open an EVENING SCHOOL for the purpose of instructing Children of Colour, as he intends, for the accommodation of some of his Employers, to exclude all Children of Colour from his Day School.

The Evening School will commence at an hour by Sun. When the white children leave the House, those of colour will take their places, and continue until ten o'clock.

The terms of teaching the white children will be as usual, two and a half dollars per quarter; those of colour, one dollar and three quarters. In both cases, the whole of the money to be paid in advance to Mr. Benjamin S. King. Those who produce Certificates from him of their having paid the money, will be admitted.

Those who think proper to put their Children under his care, may rely upon the strictest attention being paid, not only to their Education but to their Morals, which he deems an *important* part of Education.

August 23, 1808

He hopes to have a better School House by the commencement of the next quarter.[8]

An announcement of Chavis's school from the *Raleigh Register*, August 23, 1808. (North Carolina Division of Archives and History, Raleigh.)

The school in Raleigh continued as late as 1830 when Joseph Gales, the Whig editor of the *Raleigh Register*, reported in the April 1830 edition:

> On Friday last,...we attended an examination of the free
> children of colour, attached to the school conducted by
> *John Chavis*, also colored, but a regularly educated Presby-
> terian minister...
>
> To witness a well regulated school, composed of this
> class of persons—to see them setting an example both in
> behavior and scholarship, which their *white* superiors
> might take pride in imitating, was a cheering spectacle to a
> philanthropist. The exercises throughout, evinced a degree
> of attention and assiduous care on the part of the instruc-
> tor, highly creditable, and of attainment on the part of his
> scholars almost incredible.[9]

Gales was very impressed with Chavis's "well-regulated" school.
According to Gales, Chavis taught his "coloured" students that
although they were in a subordinate position in society, they were
to try to improve themselves and get a good education. He was concerned just as much for the development of their character as for
their academic achievement.

This description of Chavis's school shows the degree to which
he had to accommodate the "inspection" of his school by the white
editor. He had to wear the mask of accommodation in order to continue his teaching mission.

Ironically, within a year of this elaborate praise of his school,
Chavis would be forbidden to preach and teach as a result of laws
passed in the wake of the Nat Turner insurrection.

Before that terrible blow to his career, however, Chavis operated classical schools in Chatham, Wake, Orange, and Granville
counties. According to Shaw, "His school served as a high school
and academy for the section in which it was located, and prepared
students for the University of North Carolina."[10] During the late
middle years of his life he "taught school near Rogers Store in Barton's Creek District" of Wake County.[11] Rogers Store still stands in
northern Wake County off highway 98 going towards Durham. It is
now owned by the Rays and is called Ray's Store. According to Mrs.
Ray at the store, "It was moved from the intersection of 98 and
Rogers Store road to its present location." Across the street from
Rogers Store is the Rogers Store Post Office where John Chavis sent
mail to Senator Willie Mangum and other friends during the nineteenth century. This is the area where John Chavis lived, owned property, and taught for a number of years. Mrs. Mildred Harris, an
elderly lady of Bahama, North Carolina (the town near Senator's

Top: Rogers's Store in Northern Wake County, now called Ray's Store. *Bottom:* Rogers's Store Post Office which is now across the street from the former Rogers's Store.

Mangum's plantation), has said that Chavis used to live at Rogers Store.[12]

"After 1831 he was permitted by law to instruct only white pupils, a state law having been enacted in that year prohibiting the teaching of free Negroes or slaves."[13] However, after 1831 John Chavis taught white pupils only to a limited degree. Because white parents for the most part stopped sending their sons and daughters to him, he was in a very low economic state. He urged Willie P. Mangum, his former student and friend, to send his daughter to his school, but for a long period of time his letters went unanswered.

Nevertheless, at the height of John Chavis's teaching career, he taught many prominent North Carolinians and prepared them to enter college: Willie P. Mangum, who became a U.S. senator and president of the U.S. Senate; Senator Mangum's brother, Priestley Hinton Mangum, who became a lawyer; Archibald E. and John L. Henderson, sons of Chief Justice Henderson; Governor Charles Manly; Rev. William Harris; Dr. James L. Wortham; the Edwardses, the Enlows [Enloes], and the Hargroves.[14] Another one of Chavis's famous students was Abram Rencher, who became U.S. minister to Portugal and territorial governor of New Mexico. According to Smith:

> Many of his students became prominent as politicians, lawyers, preachers, physicians, and teachers. Prof. J. H. Horner, principal of Horner School, Oxford [Horner Military Academy], one of the oldest and best high schools in the State, in a letter of May 14, 1883, says: "He had a well attended classical school in Wake County. My father not only went to school to him but boarded in his family." He says that what his father knew he got at this school, and adds that, "Chavis was no doubt a good scholar and a good teacher, and hence was patronized by the best people of the country." The school was the best at that time to be found in the State.[15]

The above description attests to the respect the white aristocrats had for Chavis as well as for his classical learning.

As mentioned previously, Chavis wanted Mangum to send his daughter Sally to attend his school at Rogers Store, which was located at Reavis Crossroads. He also invited Mangum to visit his school there. Many facts about Chavis's life are revealed in the letters which he wrote Mangum as well as other friends and former students. Edgar Knight reports that on December 18, 1827, Chavis wrote to Willie P. Mangum, "I would thank you to attend my next examination in Wake. It will be at Reavis Crossroads where you were once on the last Thursday in July."[16] The location of Chavis's school coincides with Dr. Shaw's study of Chavis, in which he places Reavis Crossroads, the location of Chavis's home, to be nine miles from Oxford. Mrs. Sarah Young, who informed Shaw that her great grandmother Lottie Chavis was the mother of John Chavis, also stated that he lived and was born at Reavis Crossroads, which according to Shaw is also about 20 miles from Old Providence Road in the Tar River section.[17]

John Chavis's students boarded in his home at Reavis Crossroads. He taught Greek, Latin, mathematics, and English grammar. He was particularly fond of Lindley Murray's spelling book and Murray's theory about teaching English. In 1831 when he was forbidden to preach or teach, he wrote to Senator Mangum, desiring to teach the Mangum children the theory of the English language that he had learned from Murray:

> Please to give my best respect to Mrs. Mangum & tell her that I am the same old two & sixpence towards her & her children, & that she need not think it strange, that I should say, that her children will never be taught the Theory of the English Language unless I teach them. I say no still, I learnt my Theory from Lindley Murray's spelling book which no other teacher in this part of the country teaches but myself & I think it preferable to the English Grammar.[18]

Lindley Murray's grammar did not just drill in English grammar but taught composition and grammar together. Murray taught the connection between syntax (grammatical sentence structure) and ideas. He also began the study of the American spelling of English words.[19]

Chavis admired Murray's grammar of the English language and adopted it as a text because it emphasized composition in the English language. In the old Latin grammar schools, students spent a great deal of time composing essays in Latin or other foreign languages. Chavis perhaps was one of the first teachers to emphasize English composition and Murray's theory of language. Some of the ideas which Murray espoused are being revitalized today as a result of a massive decline in students' ability to write. Educators are discovering principles that Murray put forth in the nineteenth century:

> All that regards the study of composition, merits the
> higher attention upon this account, that it is intimately
> connected with the improvement of our intellectual powers.
> For I must be allowed to say, that when we are employed
> after a proper manner, in the study of composition, we are
> cultivating the understanding itself. The study of arranging
> our thoughts with propriety, teaches us to think as well as
> to speak, accurately.[20]

John Chavis also sought through his teaching to avoid "every
example and illustration" that might have an improper effect on the
minds of youth. Proper education contributed to the order and happiness of society, "by guarding the innocence and cherishing the
virtue of the rising generation."[21] Because of its religious connection, education during the eighteenth and nineteenth centuries prepared the mind to be pure and humble and the individual to receive
not only material happiness in the pursuit of life, but eternal happiness in the life to come. There was an emphasis upon piety and
social responsibility in the learning process. In the prefaces to textbooks of the nineteenth century similar to Murray's, one finds that
texts appeal not only to the intellectual development of the individual but to the moral and spiritual development of youth.

Even when teaching science, teachers of the nineteenth century
expressed a unity between science and religion. The emphasis was
on developing reverence and respect for God and spiritual matters
while learning about the mysteries of the universe. Pattillo in his
Geographical Catechism, speaking about comets, says:

> No part of God's works that have come to my knowl-
> edge, astonish me more than the infinite wisdom, fore-
> knowledge and devine art of the Deity, in throwing from
> his creating hand more than 40 enormous globes, whose
> paths oppose and cross each other for thousands of years,
> in every direction, without the rapid fiery comet once
> touching or interrupting a single planet, which must have
> frequently happened had the planet been in that part of its
> orbit in which it was before the comet passed, or would be
> soon after. Adore ye sons of men, and in humble gratitude
> acknowledge the power, wisdom and goodness of God![22]

As seen above, not only did John Chavis teach English grammar, composition, spelling, and arithmetic, but he also taught Latin
and Greek. The requirements for admission to college were based

upon the curriculum of the Latin grammar school. Students had to be examined on these subjects before being admitted to college.

As final testament to Chavis's contributions as a teacher, W. H. Ruffner, who was state superintendent of instruction in North Carolina from 1896 to 1898, writes:

> It was within the limits of this county* that Rev. John Chavis, a free man of color, taught a classical school about seventy years ago. He was a preacher in the Presbyterian Church and was highly regarded by the best men of the community, both as a teacher and as a man. Among his pupils were Willie P. Mangum and other best citizens of Orange.[23]

Ruffner is referring to Durham County, which was formed in 1881 from Orange and Wake.

CHAPTER 5

Mentor, Confidant, and Astute Business Man

By studying John Chavis's letters to his students, one gains an understanding of his character as a teacher as well as the man himself. The letters reveal that he followed the activities of his students throughout their lives, paying attention to their political careers, their financial successes and failures, and their personal lives. His students also helped him financially support his school and other business matters. Most revealing are the many letters which he sent Senator Willie P. Mangum as well as letters to Colonel George Wortham and state treasurer John Haywood.

Through the investigation of property deeds, one also sees that Chavis became prosperous through the buying and selling of land. Like his forebears, he considered land to be a valuable asset to obtaining a comfortable and prosperous living. He was one who apparently loved the land, for his students report that he was very knowledgeable about agriculture.

In short, documentary evidence supports the assertion that Chavis was a mentor, confidant, and astute business man at the height of his career.

The earliest existing Chavis letter is dated October 1817, written to John Haywood, Esq., who was treasurer of North Carolina. John Chavis had gone to visit him near his home. Not seeing him, he went to the state house. Not finding him there, he went to the bank and left money for Haywood. The letter is apparently written hurriedly. Chavis promised Haywood that he would return within "two weeks between nine and eleven o'clock."[1] This letter indicates that Chavis got around well during this period and untiringly attended to business matters.

Recorded with the Willie P. Mangum papers is another letter Chavis wrote to John Haywood, this one on July 3, 1822, in which he promises Haywood to pay a loan which he wants to renew. Chavis expresses his fear that Haywood has lost the note and assessments sent earlier, and he encloses another copy for Haywood.[2]

On January 28, 1825, Chavis writes from Raleigh to Willie P. Mangum who in that decade was serving in Congress. He informs Mangum that Captain Pullen, who apparently was responsible for collecting debts, had misrepresented Mangum's intention to pay them. Mangum and Haywood had promised to pay the debt for Chavis. Pullen apparently had been harsh with Chavis in asking "what [he] intend[s] to do about the business." However, Chavis later talked with Mangum and ameliorated the complaint which Pullen had made:

> Shortly after I conversed with Mr. Pullen I saw, & conversed with the Treasurer upon the subject, & his conversation was that of a father to a beloved son which melted my heart with thankfulness and penitential sorrow.[3]

In this same letter Chavis mentions that he is without a school and doesn't know what to do. With piety and resolute optimism, he says, "I hope however that God has in reserve some way of relief. It is commonly said that the darkest time is just before day.—"

Willie Person Mangum, a friend and former student of John Chavis. Mangum served in both the House and the Senate. Engraving by E.G. Williams and Brothers, New York, from a portrait by James R. Lambkin of Philadelphia. (Noble Papers, Southern Historical Collection, Wilson Library, University of North Carolina at Chapel Hill.)

This letter also expresses Chavis's political concerns. He is very anxious about the presidency and wants "Mr. Crawford" to be elected. He is soliciting Mangum's support for Crawford. He acknowledges that several persons will not support Mangum for reelection to the Congress if he supports Crawford, but Chavis declares that he himself will vote for Mangum. Chavis also observes the activities of the American Colonization Society and wants to know if their managers have made any propositions to Congress. Finally, he expresses his greatest concern: the growing political power of General Andrew Jackson. Apparently Chavis felt that Jackson was unfit to become president for many reasons, the most obvious being that Jackson wanted to nullify the U.S. Bank, to oppose the tariff, and to take land away from the American Indians.

In other letters we can see that Chavis had to take care of matters at home such as his school and the care of livestock, not only of his own but of his friends. On July 1, 1825, he writes to Paul Cameron from Orange County and informs him that he has been teaching school near the Eno Baptist Meeting House in Orange County. He gives suggestions on how Cameron might prevent a raging disease among the cattle, especially the cows. He probably gained a knowledge of natural medicines from his ancestors. For this fatal type of distemper that affected the cattle, Chavis suggests the following as a preventative.

> Hickory sapling should be cut in the spring and burnt to ashes & these should be sprinkled in your Salt, Troughs, & sprinkle your salt on them, & let your cattle lick them. They being of a slopping nature, will cause ease of digestion, & which will prevent the distemper taking place. Although the spring is over, yet I should suppose the lateness of the season, ought not to prevent the experiment's being made. This information I recv'd from a _____ who had suffered much by this disease among his cattle & since he used the ashes he never lost a cow & his neighbor's cattle [&] horses died around his plantation....[4]

He also gives Cameron a suggestion for curing a human illness, a type of stomach sickness: "I also mentioned the use of weak Sage for the belly." It is to be "given by drinking." A "respectable lady had recommended it and had also given it to her children."

Chavis also states in this letter that his prospects for having a school in this area of Orange County are better than they have been for eight years past, but that he is suffering from rheumatism which he has "laboured under for 30 years [and which] has brought me to my crutches." He is assured of the fact that had it not been for God he would have quit his school. He hopes that "by the use of these [remedies] and the application of strong vinegar and salt, I shall be able to continue my school. I have in my school 2 families from upwards of twenty years down to six & my scholars make excellent proficiency, for which I am thankful."[5] It is interesting to see the various age levels which Chavis taught. Despite the differences in their ages, each student achieved proficiency due to the individual attention that Chavis gave.

In closing this letter Chavis asks that Cameron be favorable to Mangum's reelection to Congress: "I hope you are friendly to Judge Mangum's election. I think him one of the greatest men on the floor of the Congress." Again he demonstrates his concern for not only the personal welfare of his students and their physical well being but for their political achievement in the service of their country.

So concerned is he about Willie P. Mangum's remaining in office and not alienating his constituents that he writes to Mangum on November 20, 1825, telling him that it would be improper for the government to recognize the Haitian government. However, he states that if the president of the United States mentions it in his message, "it would be well for Congress to pass it in silence and not agitate it as a question at all & this I should suppose could be managed out of doors."[6]

In the same letter he expresses a desire to have a school in Wake County and also in Hillsborough (in Orange County), because he wants to discontinue the school in Ellerbie's (Ellerbe's) Creek. Like most of his letters, this one centers around politics and the development of his schools.

In another letter Chavis shows his acquaintance with people in authority in North Carolina who would be beneficial to Mangum's career and might also help with his own financial problems. He wants to buy property owned by a Mr. Rogers in the Barton Creek area of Wake County and to move from his present house to this new location. He asks Mangum if he would draw up the deed for the land, because he wants to get out "of the miserable hut" he is in before Christmas. He promises Mangum that he will send him a description of the land and asks Mangum to send his replies to Mangum's father's house. Therefore this letter indicates that Chavis visited Mangum's father's house, which was on the Mangum plantation.[7]

(We will return to a discussion of Mangum's father's house in the last chapter, "The Search for the Gravesite.")

On March 11, 1828, Chavis writes Mangum another letter which indicates that Mangum had not answered his previous letter in regards to writing the deed for the Rogers's land. Chavis first describes the land, then repeats his request to the senator:

> One hundred acres more or less, bounded on the South
> by Solomon Thompson, and Jacob Hunter, on the West by
> the Lands of James Boyd, on the North by Richard Smith,
> & on the East by Tignal Jones, the Land is well timbered
> with pine oak & other common growth known by the
> name of the Job Rogers Tract, to be given to me during life
> & during the life of my wife Frances or her widowhood—If
> your engagements should be such that you cannot write the
> deed, & send it by Mr. Jones; please to write it & bring it
> to Wake Superior Court & send it by him or some of our
> neighbors, the Thompsons or the Rogers or others.[8]

In this letter he also tells Mangum to give his respects "to my sons Abram & Priestley (Abraham Rencher and Mangum's brother Priestley) & tell them I never expect to see them again, unless they should condescend to come to see me." He needs financial and moral support at this time. He has a school of 16 students which "may probably arrive at 20; however the people are very mulish."

> I am very anxious respecting your affairs. I fear John J.
> will injure you from report. But I hope strict attention to
> the practice of Law will relieve you, & that you will be
> enabled to lay up for your family. I hope also that you have
> given out all thoughts of moving to Hillsborough. My
> respects to Mrs. Mangum & believe me to be yours with
> all my heart. [9]

Due to financial exigencies, an indenture of Willie P. Mangum to James Webb and Thomas D. Watts of Orange County, North Carolina, is made on April 25, 1828. In this indenture Mangum mortgages all of his land and slaves except for the new house which his family lives in to Webb and Watts for the payment of debts. These lands, amounting to 1600 acres, were inherited by Willie P. Mangum from his grandfather Arthur Mangum. The conveyance made to Webb and Watts is executed to indemnify debts and a bank note which Mangum owes to the Bank of North Carolina. The note is endorsed by Duncan Cameron.[10]

On the following day, April 26, 1828, a warrant is issued by the justice of the peace of Orange County, John L. Carrington, against Willie P. Mangum and Walter A. Mangum for the amount of $69.87. Robert Cozart was the plaintiff. The warrant was received by James Webb, trustee of the Mangum estate.[11]

Less than a year later Mangum's mother died. On March 12, 1829, a letter was sent from W. M. Green in Hillsborough to Willie P. Mangum, informing him that his mother had died on the previous Tuesday morning of bilious colic.[12] At this time Mangum is not in Washington but is serving as a judge at the Ashe Court House and in Morganton, North Carolina.

Chavis writes to Mangum (now a U.S. senator) on September 3, 1831, three years after his last letter. It is possible that other letters written between 1828 and 1831 have been lost. The tone of this letter is more desperate and bitter than the previous one. Chavis cannot understand why Mangum and his other white friends have neither answered his letters nor given him any attention:

> Is it my colour, or my insignificance or the gross ignorance, which my many letters contain, the reason why you have never condescended to answer one of them? Or is it your distrust of my professed, firm, unshaken, unabating friendship for you & your family? Or do you consider my friendship to be not worth your notice? Be it as it may, I must plainly & honestly tell you that I have even been grieved, that you were the professed political friend of G. Jackson, because I ever believed him to be expressly what he has proved to be.... You as an honest statesman can not keep sides with him any longer, therefore put on again your full coat of Federalism, & not only support the election of Clay, but go forth to Congress with a full determination to support the renewal of the United States bank, to trample under foot the doctrine of Nullification, to support Internal improvements, in a word to prove that you are an American in the full sense of the word.[13]

At the beginning of this letter Chavis admonishes his former student for ignoring his letters, but the concern for himself is overshadowed by his concern for Mangum as a political leader who is being drawn into the camp of General Jackson. He opposes Jackson and supports Henry Clay because Jackson wants to nullify the U.S. Bank and opposes the tariff upon imports and the building of the infrastructure of the country.

Chavis uses a very witty description of Mangum's irresolute political behavior:

> I have told you to put on your Federalism again. You know that you have been for some time past, hoping [sic] & shifting about, showing your coat, to be sometimes Federalism, sometimes Democracy, sometimes Republicanism. Now you know this won't do, because you know that no political stratagem whatever can shake the foundation of Federalism.[14]

Here Chavis talks to Mangum as a father to his son. He chastises him with love. These words indicate Chavis's strong feelings for Federalism and the centralization of governmental powers. His strong beliefs in the powers of the federal government are a result of his educational background, which stressed the principles of the Declaration of Independence.

Chavis refers in the same letter to "this Potter business." Robert Potter from Granville County had castrated a black man because the man was accused of having intercourse with Potter's wife. Chavis considered this act wholly uncalled for and as violent as the punishment given those in the Nat Turner insurrection:

> But oh this Potter business was ever the like done before—guilty or not guilty? Please to drop us a line by Mr. Devereux & let us know the beginning & the effect, for the reports are as various here, as that abominable insurrection in Southampton, was in its outset. For my part I cannot believe that either of the parties are guilty.[15]

Even though he refers to the Nat Turner insurrection as abominable, he closes by implying that neither the black man who was castrated nor the principal characters in the insurrection were guilty.

In the same letter Chavis expresses regret that Mangum's brother, Priestley, did not win the election. He points to Priestley's stubbornness as a pitfall to his political career:

> I see, my son Priestley as I expected is not elected. Yes & you may tell from me, that unless he lay aside that stubborn unyielding disposition of his & become condescending & familiar he will never set the River on fire, neither for himself or his children.[16]

Mangum early in the following year writes to his wife, Charity A. Mangum, that he received her letter and a letter from Chavis on the same date. From the letter it appears that Mangum was not aware that Sally, his daughter, was not in school.

> I regret very much that Sally is not at school. I still think that Hinton did not act well toward me. As to the complaint in the neighborhood, it is ridiculous; & he had nothing to do but to act in such a way as to put it down. I have been thinking a good deal upon the subject. Mr. Chavis made a proposition to me; but being from home, I cannot do anything in it.[17]

In the letter Mangum further explains that sending Sally to Chavis's school would be too costly and that he will send her as a day scholar to a school in the neighborhood. At Chavis's school in northern Wake County, male students boarded at his house, and Chavis had recommended that Sally stay at a respectable woman's house near his school.

Chavis writes another letter to Mangum. Apparently he has not received a letter from Mangum yet, although Mangum had already replied to Mrs. Mangum's letter. Chavis is not aware that Mangum will not be able to send his children to school. The letter also reveals that Chavis and Mrs. Mangum were together at Mangum's home when both of them wrote a letter to the senator. Chavis writes,

> It is four weeks today since I left your house, at which time, Mrs. Mangum & myself wrote to you respecting my teaching School for you. It was agreed also, that as soon as Mrs. Mangum received your answer, she was to write to me. I promised her also, that I would not engage to teach for any person nor persons until I rec'd a letter from her.... At any rate, I expected that if you disapproved of my terms, that you write to Mrs. Mangum to make me a proposition and it may be done, as no letters have come to hand—
>
> So anxious am I to teach your children the Theory of the English Language, that I am truly sorry that I had not told Mrs. Mangum to write to you, (or written so myself) that if nothing else could be done, that w'd come & Teach Sally alone, for the same you w'd have to give for her board in Hillsborough, provided you w'd board me & let me have a horse occasionally [to go] & see my family....

> I fear that my promise to Mrs. Mangum will prevent me
> from getting a school at all, for I put off all attempts to this
> day, but I must set out on Monday to see what I can do, &
> if sh'd be disappointed, I have stated what I will do for you
> so that I shall expect an answer to this letter to be left at
> the post office of Rogers's Store—[18]

One notices how urgently Chavis wanted to teach the Mangum children, and yet it would never be a possibility. He was not aware of Mangum's financial difficulties and the great resistance the whites were mounting against blacks' teaching after the Nat Turner insurrection. Shortly afterwards this problem would face him more directly.

This letter reveals that Chavis had a family, not just a wife, and shows Chavis's willingness to leave his family for a period of time to stay at the Mangum's house and teach the Mangum children. However, John Chavis's wife, Frances, did not agree with his going to stay with Mrs. Mangum. Frances apparently was the prop behind John. According to reports made by the children of John's students, she kept the house and his clothes immaculately clean. The white students who boarded at her house apparently were pleased with her culinary and domestic art.

Rogers's Store was the community where Chavis lived. It is located in the Barton Creek area near present day Leesville. As mentioned above, the store itself, according to the present day owner whose last name is Ray, was moved from the intersection of 98 going west toward Durham County to its present location. The building retains its old section where John Chavis traded and bought agricultural implements, other merchandise, and supplies of food. There is a long solid pine counter, and around the walls hang harnesses and other old implements. The old post office is across the street from the store. One wonders what old letters and papers might still be found in the post office, which is now an abandoned building.

Chavis in the letter of March 10, 1832, expresses his admiration for Henry Clay's eloquence and his fervent support for the United States Bank and the extension of the tariff. He closes by admonishing Senator Mangum, his former student:

> Please to give my respects to my son—Abraham Rencher
> & to Gen. Barringer—& tell them I w'd be glad to receive a
> letter from them. Tell them if I am Black I am free born

American & a revolutionary soldier & therefore ought not
to be thrown intirely out of the scale of notice.

> I am your Ob't. Hb. Sv't
> John Chavis[19]

The above statement verifies that Chavis was a free black American
and that he fought in the Revolutionary War.

It is now July 21, 1832, and Chavis still has not received a reply
from Mangum regarding his teaching Sally. He asks Mangum to
speak to Colonel Horner about sending his daughter Juliana to be
taught by him. He says that he will only charge "at three or three
& a half dollars a month at most the tuition eight dollars." In his
customary fashion, he switches from his own interest in maintaining his school to the welfare of the country. He admonishes Mangum
for favoring the election of General Jackson for the presidency.
Finally, he informs Mangum that he did not buy the land from Benjamin Rogers.

> I have the satisfaction to tell you, that Benj'n Rogers has,
> of his own accord become as friendly as ever he was. What
> wrought the change in him I cant tell. There has been no
> sale, & I expect will not be.[20]

Seemingly with some feeling of desperation, Chavis laments:

> My respects to Mrs. Mangum & tell her never expect to
> see her at her house any more or again. If you will write
> direct your letter to be left at the post office at Rogers's
> store—[21]

On August 8, 1832, Chavis writes again to Willie P. Mangum.
This letter is in a happier mood, for the venerable teacher has finally
received a letter from the senator. However, he upbraids Mangum
for implying in his letter that to be a genuine Federalist would be
unsound in politics. Chavis has such a firm belief in Federalism that
he cannot foresee the coming cleavage in national politics. Chavis
firmly denounces anti–Federalism:

> I do not believe that mankind are capable of living under,
> either a Democratic or a Republican Government. The
> bonds of such Governments are not sufficient to restrain
> the corruptions of human nature. The volcano will burst,
> & the lava spread far and wide its destructive ruins.[22]

He firmly believes that General Jackson does not have the dignity or character to rule the nation: "the reasons which G.J. gave for puting [sic] his Veto on the bank bill was not worth a gourd button."

At the end of the letter Chavis expresses his joy at learning that Mrs. Mangum has had another child. He still suggests that Sally can board at Mrs. Solomon Thompson's house and attend his school. Finally, still thinking of the future of Mangum's family, he tells the senator, "Mrs. Tignal Jones alias Amelia ... has requested me to give her respects to Mrs. Mangum & tell her that she has three sons ... to match her daughters."[23]

Chavis writes to Mangum again on September 24, 1832, explaining in detail his position respecting the tariff, the bank vote and the presidency. He writes again on October 1, 1832, to inform Mangum that Mr. John Hunt of "Greenville" [Granville] has made a resolution to support him and his wife during life and has appointed a committee to make arrangements for that purpose. Chavis appreciates the offer because he has become financially burdened as a result of not operating his school. This letter shows that although he has the support from the Presbytery, he still wants his patrons to support his school:

> I told Mr. Hunt that I was thankful & would accept ... the offer, but that I was in debt, and could not go until next fall or winter—that I thought I had a prospect of making a school for the next year which w'd be sufficient to cover all my debts provided my neighbors would patronize me as they ought to do. But should they not, I wish you to know that I will Teach for you the next year provided you can make such a school as will justify me to leave my family to take care of themselves.
>
> You are to recollect that school must not exceed a quarter of a mile from your door & let it be less if possible & your payments must be at least half yearly. The school to commence on the first Monday in Jan'y.[24]

Writing to Mangum on November 3, 1832, he is pleased that Mangum's friends are attacking Mangum's opponents. Chavis himself attacks Albemarle and Iredell, who supported nullification of the United States Bank. He is especially tormented because Mangum's opponents are calling Mangum names. Again like a father, he feels that he can attack Mangum for his political errors, but he doesn't want others to do so:

To hear you traduced is killing. I can blame and scold
you myself but I don't like other people to do it. [25]

He despises the idea that Mangum will go to Washington and vote
for General Jackson:

> Let him take G. J. From his crad[le] up to his reappoint-
> ing Guin to the Secretary office of the sale of the Indians
> Lands & see if he cannot discover—a host of blots of the
> deepest dye in his character—undeserving a chief Magis-
> trate?[26]

In a letter to his wife, Charity, dated December 15, 1832, Senator Mangum expresses his discouragement about the behavior of
the newly elected President Jackson. Chavis had tried to warn
Mangum about the candidate beforehand. Mangum writes,

> The weak and foolish Cabinet of the President has
> undone all the good that we hoped from his message. The
> whole concern is deficient in talent and good practical
> sense. His proclamation is violent & dangerous in its prin-
> ciples.[27]

Therefore Mangum begins taking a stand against Jackson's policies.
At this turn of events, Chavis is elated. He writes to Mangum from
Wake County:

> I am perfectly satisfied and do rejoice that I can speak to
> my neighbors with freedom & confidence respecting the
> course of my friend Judge Mangum—
> Mr. Brown ought to be at home grubbing or frying pan-
> cakes for his wife (if he has got one) instead of having a
> seat in the Senate of the United States—[28]

In his notes to the collection of the Mangum Papers, Henry Thomas
Shanks writes,

> In the heated debate that continued for the first three
> months of 1834, Mangum said little. On January 23 he
> presented memorials of "sundry citizens" of the state. Later
> he added those from Burke, Fayetteville, Wilkes, Washing-
> ton, and Lenoir. On February 25 he made his main speech
> against the removal of deposits. The "Young Men" of

Hartford, Connecticut, published it in pamphlet form. After denying Senator Brown's contention that the memorials did not represent the sentiment in North Carolina, Mangum made a strong attack on Jackson for deserting the South on the tariff. He condemned those who blindly followed the President. Finally he emphasized the unconstitutionality of removal of the deposits. The money, he said, was placed by law in the U.S. Bank and Jackson had removed it for the gain of his supporters.[29]

Chavis felt gratified that his friend and former student was more enlightened about Jacksonian politics; however, Chavis's financial problems prevented him from concentrating on Mangum's accomplishments. In the previous letter, dated February 26, 1834, from Chavis to Mangum, one sees the pitiable financial state of the elderly teacher and his wife. He complains:

> Last year I made about $30 by teaching & this year, perhaps I may 6 [*paper torn*]. Thus you see what a miserable neighborhood I live in—
> My wife has been dying slowly for about fifteen months. She is not completely comfortable [in] her bed, but has not been found of disadvantage to the family during [*several lines are faded*].[30]

Although his wife Frances was deathly ill during this period, John would precede her in death just four years later. It is to be noted that he mentions the family again in this letter and that they were attentive to his wife during her illness.

Not only was John Chavis a mentor and confidant of his former students and his political associates, but he had a business life of his own. During the height of his career, he became prosperous through the buying and selling of land. In 1800, his brother Jordan Chavis, Sr., had bought land from John Freeman on the east side of Mine Creek in Raleigh. In 1805 Jordan Chavis sold the same land to John Chavis for one hundred dollars, at total of 25 acres. In 1806 Joshua Eastland also sold John Chavis land adjoining the latter's newly acquired tract for $700: "Beginning at a point at Isaac Hunter, Sr.'s line to Big Bear Branch and also to Mine Creek, and from Mine Creek to Cool Branch, a total of 233 acres."[31]

Also in 1806 Abel Olive sold Elias Bowden the land which Silas High later sold to John Chavis in 1811. In 1807 John Chavis had sold his land east of Mine Creek to Abel Olive for $700. Then Abel Olive sold the same property to Jesse Olive and Elias Bowden for $700.[32] Thus one sees that John Chavis and a circle of friends bought and exchanged property with one another, sometimes using the same money over and over again.

In 1811 Silas High sold to John Chavis for five hundred silver minted dollars land adjoining Peyton High on Crabtree Creek, consisting of 100 acres. In 1813 Peyton High sold to John Chavis for $287 on the waters of Crabtree adjoining "where the said John Cheves now lives ... consisting of 5 acres and three quarters." [33] Two years later on June 28, 1815, W. E. Roberts sold to John Chavis for fifty pounds property on "the South Side of the Neuse River on the waters of Laurel Creek containing one hundred and eleven acres, beginning at Red Oak on Samuel Reavis' land."[34]

One wonders where Chavis acquired the money to purchase these vast areas of land. Perhaps he acquired wealth from preaching and teaching as well as through certain business arrangements with his friends, such as Senator Mangum and Treasurer Heyward. It is also curious to note how fast property changed hands. During the same year of 1815, on July 1, Chavis sold the land back to William E. Roberts for indebtedness of $170 and the land was sold to William Holloway. However, the deed was not recorded until 1822.[35]

We hear of John Chavis's property again only through his heirs. Questions remain: Why did he acquire large tracts of land, and how did he lose his property? The amount of land he acquired suggests that he had a large family. He apparently acquired the land to support his family, which included his children and other relatives. A deed dated July 5, 1870, titled Gatsey Mitchell vs. Wm. Chavis Heirs, states:

> The undersigned to whom to us referred the matter of Gatsey Mitchell, wife of Alfred Mitchell and the heirs at Law of Wm.[William] Chavis, as to the interest which they ... either of them have in Lot No. 46 in the City of Raleigh which Lot was the estate of Sallie Chavis, deceased have ... the same and from the testimony are of opinion ... that John Chavis was born in lawful wedlock and that he was the son of Wm. Chavis and Sallie Small his wife: That the children of the said John Chavis, to wit: John Chavis, Sallie Chavis, and Lizzie, wife of Jackson Alston are joint heirs at law with Gatsey Mitchell & Sallie Chavis and as such are tenants in common of said Lot No. 46....

> Gatsey Mitchell is entitled to one full half of said Lot,
> and the said children of John Chavis are entitled to the
> other half of said Lot. They further award that the costs of
> this ... be paid, the one half by Gatsey Mitchell and the
> other half by the heirs of John Chavis. July 5, 1870.[36]

Gatsey Mitchell's maiden name was Gatsey Chavis.

The property (Lot 46 in the city of Raleigh) is described in a later deed as on the corner of East Cabarrus Street and Person Street.[37] An elderly lady in Raleigh, when asked if she knew anything about Lot 46, replied, "That was where the teacher lived."[38]

This 1870 deed further authenticates the fact that John Chavis had children. He was the son of William Chavis. It is also possible that Sarah (sometimes called Sallie) Small had the middle name of Lottie. As mentioned in Chapter I, Mrs. Sarah Young, whom Dr. G. C. Shaw refers to in his biography of John Chavis, says that John Chavis was the son of her great-grandmother Lottie Chavis. It is noted that Sarah Young also bears the name *Sarah*. Elizabeth Hummel's book on marriage bonds in Granville County shows that John Chavis was a bondsman for the marriage of his mother, Lottie Chavis, to Littleton Tabon. The marriage bond was made on April 14, 1818 (Bond No. 1020).[39] Two years earlier John Chavis had been the bondsman for the marriage of Abraham Anderson and Polly Bass, on April 24, 1816. A year before that he had married Sarah Frances Anderson on June 8, 1815. Abraham Anderson in turn was the bondsman for John Chavis' marriage.[40] As mentioned before, many of these marriages took place many years earlier. The dates are close, it is possible that there was a compelling legal reason at these late dates to post the marriage bonds. To further verify Mrs. Sarah Young's statement about John Chavis, Peggy Chavis, whom Mrs. Young mentions as her grandmother, is listed under the estate of Phillip Chavis, who was the grandfather of John Chavis.[41]

Such was the varied life of Chavis as mentor, confidant, and business man before his life's history was clouded by oppression and mystery.

CHAPTER 6

Saga of the Chavis Family

There was a time when three-fourths of the land in southern Virginia and northern North Carolina belonged to John Chavis's ancestors. Records indicate that his great grandfather, William Chavis, sold land to many of the White settlers.[1] The history of the Chavis family is closely related to the meeting and intermingling of the three dominant races of America during the colonial period: the Native Americans, the Africans, and the Caucasians, as well as to the development of the early counties of North Carolina. As seen in Chapter One, Phillip Chavis had inherited from his father, William Chavis, the land which was given to him and his father by the Earl of Granville, John Carteret, who was secretary to King George II in 1761.

Subsequently, however, after William's death when Phillip had inherited his father's land in 1778, the notoriously corrupt Reuben Searcy, the Granville County sheriff, imposed great fines upon Phillip, claiming that the latter had trespassed upon Asa Tiner's land. Searcy was an official of the British Administration, a holdover from pre–Revolutionary days, and his corruption is well documented by other writers. Officials like Searcy often imposed heavy fines on landowners as a form of extortion or a means of obtaining their property.[2] Because of these fines, Phillip was forced to sell Tiner (his brother-in-law) a great portion of the property which he had inherited from his father. Phillip had to pay the court five hundred pounds, which Searcy and Tiner probably shared. Then on November 6, 1780, Phillip was charged again with trespassing on Tiner's land and this time was charged the amount of five hundred thousand pounds. (See Appendix A for copies of relevant documents.)

Phillip's father, William, had resided in Old Bute County, which had been formed from Granville County as mentioned in Chapter One. As early as May 1770, he had trouble from Asa Tiner (sometimes spelled Tyner), his son-in-law, who had apparently threatened to do "bodily hurt, or damage done to his [William's] estate." As a result of William's taking him to court, Tiner had to pay him fifty pounds.[3] Subsequently, Asa Tiner brought many suits against William Chavis in court.[4] Therefore the excessive fines and suits against Phillip Chavis were a continuation of the struggle waged against his ancestors because of their influence and wealth.

Due to the heavy fines imposed upon him, Phillip had to liquidate his father's estate, selling the house and such things as dishes, pewter, china, beds, cattle, and even the family Bibles. (See Appendix A for a document on the sale of William Chavis's estate.) Also much of the land owned by the Chavises, as well as by other early settlers who had received land from the Crown, was confiscated by the state of North Carolina following the Revolution.[5]

It is interesting, however, that the name of John Chavis is on the back of a deed pertaining to land that was once owned by his ancestors. This deed, which is found in Appendix A, was given by Phillip Chavis to Richard Clopton; from Richard Clopton to Jonathan Davis; and from John Finch to Thomas White. The latter deed has John Chavis's name on the back of it. The same property exchanged hands back and forth between John, his relatives, and friends. This deed is found in the North Carolina Archives today. It reads:

> The land begins at a poplar on the bank of Tar River
> near the mouth of Collins Creek running across said Creek
> North of East 139 poles to a pine stump thence north 55
> West 45 poles to a white oak on the county line to a pine
> stump thence east 2 poles to a pine then south 160 poles to
> a red oak and Sassafras then East 104 poles to a red oak
> and hickory then South 68 poles to a white oak then South
> 82 East 148 poles to a white oak down then South 7 west
> 222 poles to a pine stump ... all totaling 200 acres.
> Deed John Finch to Thomas White, 17th. August 1785

All of these pioneers including John Chavis gave their lives for the development of this country, whether as builders, agriculturalists, soldiers, educators, preachers, or mentors. Yet their bodies are buried in anonymity as though they had never lived. No prominent stones mark the grave sites of these founders. According to Blacknall, however, there is a creek in Granville County named for Gibrea Chavis, which is called Gib's Creek.

CHAPTER 7

A Path of Fire

Many writers have noted the dearth of information concerning John Chavis's birth and early life. Many records apparently have been lost for various reasons such as wars, social upheavals, and court house fires. However, the old adage "Truth crushed to earth shall rise again" seems to be applicable to the history of John Chavis.

Many records perhaps have been lost through fires or neglect. It is noteworthy that in 1802, less than two months after Chavis completed his course of studies at the Presbyterian Washington College (first known as Liberty College) a few miles outside of Lexington, Virginia, a fire destroyed the main building, which had just been erected in 1793. The fire was "thought to be of incendiary origin."[1]

Before Washington College, Chavis studied at Princeton, yet many writers have questioned whether he attended the ivy league school. One of the few records of his having attended Princeton University is the record of the Board of Trustees cited in Chapter 2. However, Varnum Collins, the secretary of Princeton, stated that Chavis was among a few black and Indian students who studied privately under Dr. Witherspoon at Princeton.[2] Black historian Carter G. Woodson, along with many other scholars, also affirms Chavis's having attended Princeton University, where "he took rank as a good Latin and a fair Greek scholar."[3] Collins found Chavis's name listed in the winter session of 1795 of students at Princeton.

The image of fire is symbolic of the destruction of many records pertaining to Chavis as well as to the distortion of his character by some historians. Some writers have contended that he was bitterly opposed to abolition. These assertions are based upon only one letter purported to be from Chavis to Willie P. Mangum, dated November 17, 1836, in which the writer asserts that Congress had "no more right to pass a law eliminating slavery in the district than I have to go to your house and take Orange [Mangum's servant] and bring

The ruins of Liberty Hall at Washington College in Lexington, Virginia. Fire consumed the building on Christmas Eve, 1802, less than two months after John Chavis's graduation. (The Library of Virginia.)

him home and keep him as my servant," Chavis was speaking (if he wrote the letter) to Mangum as a friend and not issuing a public manifesto against abolition. Yet this statement has been blown all out of the proportion by writers such as Gossie H. Hudson.[4] Hudson refers to Chavis as an accommodationist and an "Uncle Tom." In spite of his feverish attempt to present the famous teacher in a negative way, he has failed because he has not studied Chavis's background and his relationship to Senator Mangum before drawing his conclusions.

Chavis as a teacher and mentor of Senator Mangum foresaw the confusion, depredations, and even violence that would ensue as a result of immediate abolition. Further results of immediate emancipations would be the hatred of the slaves by their masters and the exploitation of them by northern carpetbaggers. In addition, he thought that not only would immediate abolition jeopardize the welfare and security of the south, but it would erode national unity and

Federalism, which were to him the birthright of the nation. Yet Hudson attempts to psychoanalyze Chavis according to the Marxist view of the colonized vis-à-vis the colonizer. Hudson writes:

> The concept of distance, according to Wright, is not physical, but psychological. It involves a situation in which for moral or social reasons, an individual fears that there is another person above him. Yet physically ... they all live on the same plane.[5]

Such a simplistic psychoanalytical conclusion cannot be drawn about Chavis because his situation in the nineteenth century antebellum South is not analogous to twentieth century Marxist paradigms. He considered himself to be not apart from but of the warp and woof of the American republic.

An Uncle Tom is a pathetic obsequious type of person, who says, "Yes, suh" to everything his white masters say or want to do. Certainly Chavis does not fit this category. As shown in Chapter 5, he spoke boldly against the racist, immoral actions of Andrew Jackson and spoke sometimes harshly to Mangum for being what Chavis saw as a "change coat" politician. From his letters, we see that Chavis often placed his love for his country and friends above his own interests, even though he had every opportunity to do just the opposite. The following passage from a letter to Mangum further indicates that he spoke frankly and unabashedly on issues:

> P.S. I am sorry that your writer [person who had written a verbal denouncement about Albemarle] did not give Albemarle a slap of the jaws for his low lived, pitiful despotic objection to your keeping company of Federalist Adams & Clay men. He deserved not only a slap of the jaws, but a peak of the Butt.[6]

Furthermore, Chavis speaks to Mangum as a father to a son, not as a groveling inferior to a superior. When Mangum implied that Chavis's Federalist politics were unsound, Chavis upbraids him in an uncompromising manner:

> have I not often browbeaten you for your shifting conduct; And how could you have the daring impudence, to tell me, in broad open day light, that I had become unsound in my politics? Are you not a pretty handsome fellow?[7]

Chavis was concerned not only about Mangum's political development and the political development of the country, but about Mangum's economic welfare. He also prevented Mangum from engaging in a duel with a rival.

The historical record shows that Chavis was on an equal level with his peers until later in life when he became the target of political repression. Before that time, there was no social or political reason for him to envy anyone else's status. His white students looked up to him as a father, and he apparently loved them just as he called them: "My sons."

According to Ruffner, it was Stephen B. Weeks who stated that Chavis was born free in Granville County about 1763. Weeks also had informed Ruffner that Chavis was a "full blooded negro" who received "a classical education under Dr. Witherspoon at Princeton."

> He was admitted to Orange Presbytery in 1805. He preached often to whites at Shiloh, Nutbush, & Island [Creek] churches. His language was free from negroisms, & his preaching clear and interesting. He was a good Latin & Greek scholar, & taught in Granville, West Lake [Wake], Chatham, & perhaps East Orange counties.... Dr. Weeks showed me some of his letters to Senator Mangum. They prove that the Senator treated him as a friend & are well written. One of them dated in 1837 was a vigorous protest against the Petition for Emancipation, sent to Congress by the Abolitionists, as injurious to the colored race.[8]

Stephen B. Weeks was related to Senator Mangum by marriage. He married Senator Mangum's granddaughter, Sallie Leach. Along with Ashbel Green, Weeks was one of the first writers to claim that John Chavis was a full blooded Negro. He was also the first perhaps to mention the letter which was purported to be written by Chavis against the abolition vote. Interestingly, Weeks contended, according to Edgar Knight, that John Chavis did not teach Senator Mangum. Weeks said "Chavis did not have the honor" of teaching Willie P. Mangum.[9] Weeks became a well known and highly respected historian of North Carolina.

The implications of certain myths surrounding Chavis have been devastating both politically and educationally. If Chavis were a pure Negro and also without heirs, that would mean that he was not related to anyone in Granville County, past or present, and that he left no family legacy. Perpetuating the myth that he was adamantly against slavery would cut him off not only from the slaves and free blacks of his time but would present a negative picture of him for all times. However, it is hoped that the facts presented in this study will refute some of these myths and rumors which have been fostered either voluntarily or involuntarily.

As in other accounts already mentioned, especially in Chapter 1, descriptions of Chavis by people who knew him indicate that he was mixed blood. According to Captain S. Venable, "Chavis was coffee or gingerbread color—which indicated a mixture of Arab and Negro."[10] However, as explained earlier, Chavis's appearance was due to a mixture of African and North American Indian heritage. According to the accounts presented in Chapter 1, he was a descendant of William Chavis, of American Indian and "free issue" African American ancestry. Across the state of North Carolina, the oral historians of the Chavis family admit their African and Indian heritage.

Chavis knew how to appeal to his fellow Presbyterians, even though he had to mask his feelings on several occasions. Many of his fellow Presbyterians owned slaves. However, he prefaced his remarks to Mangum by saying, "Slavery is an evil institution." As a free black minister and teacher, Chavis could not free himself from the pangs of racial oppression. Laws could be enacted to disenfranchise the free blacks at the stroke of a pen. He never intended his private letters to be sounded "from the rooftops," as he relates in one of his letters.

His last letters of 1837 indicate his disgust with the laws which impeded his preaching and teaching. There is also a sense of misgiving for having written Mangum on the abolition question. He wrote Mangum that his opinion on abolition should not have had an adverse effect on "free people of colour" getting an education.[11]

Finally, Chavis's last sermon on "The Atonement," which he wished to have published in 1837, was vigorously attacked by colleagues in the Orange Presbytery. They objected to his publishing the sermon, not because it would have been uninteresting and financially unfeasible, but because he makes a strong statement in the sermon against the intolerance and bigotry of the Old School theology, which his colleagues had embraced. According to Chavis, he had been contemplating the theology surrounding the doctrine of grace and salvation for thirty years. He published his sermon without the blessings of his friends in the Presbytery, who did not cooperate in buying and circulating the sermon. In "The Atonement" Chavis symbolically not only attacks the system of inequality in the temporal world, but preaches an inclusionary grace for the equality of all human beings in the world to come. Even though Chavis's true character has been distorted by some, the fire of his wisdom and spiritual fervor vanquishes all other flames.

CHAPTER 8

Resurrection: In Search of His Gravesite

Through perseverance and deep interest, I was able to initiate what was apparently the first investigation to discover the gravesite of John Chavis. This has been a labor of love. Some historical accounts of Chavis's death are written as though he disappeared into thin air around 1838. However, G. C. Shaw was one of the first writers to state that Chavis was buried on the Willie P. Mangum estate in Rougemont, North Carolina, in Durham County. Shaw writes:

> The remains of this noble son rest about twenty miles southwest of Oxford near a little town, on the Norfolk and Western Railroad, called Rougemont. Massive cedars stand as sentinels keeping watch over the sacred spot, and tall pines, swayed by the winds, sing requiems, and luxuriant honeysuckles cover the ground for yards around. Here in the private burying ground of Mr. Willie Mangum, his staunch friend, rest the bones of John Chavis, this noble son of Nature.[1]

Some members of the newly formed John Chavis Historical Society made a first expedition to the Mangum Estate to visit the cemetery there in November 1987. Members who went on the expedition were my brother, Rev. Dr. Benjamin F. Chavis, Jr.; my cousins, Mrs. Vivian Chavis Ross of Clarksville, Virginia, and Mrs. Madelyn Pine of Nelson, Virginia; Mr. Matthew Chavis III of Maryland; Miss Octavia Chavis of Alexandria, Virginia; two photographers and I. Mr. Michael Hill, historian for the North Carolina Archives, gave me a map of Hill Forest, which is the name that the North Carolina State University School of Forestry gave to the plantation when they took control of it. According to Hill,

96

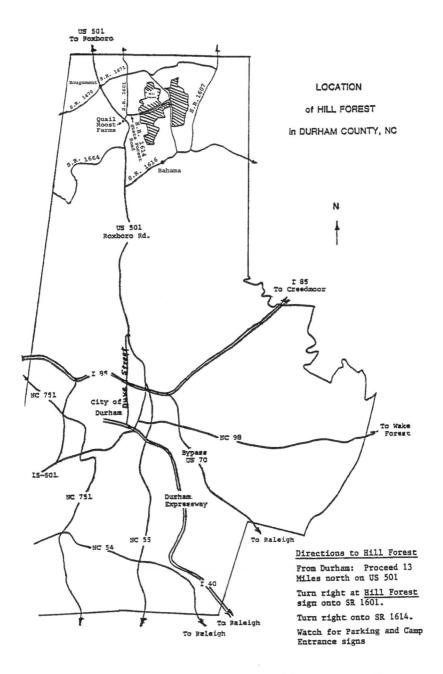

LOCATION

of HILL FOREST

in DURHAM COUNTY, NC

N

Directions to Hill Forest

From Durham: Proceed 13 Miles north on US 501

Turn right at Hill Forest sign onto SR 1601.

Turn right onto SR 1614.

Watch for Parking and Camp Entrance signs

Map to Hill Forest. The plantation once owned by Senator Willie P. Mangum is part of this forest. The burial site of John Chavis is believed to be in the Mangum family cemetery here. (N.C. State University, Department of Forestry.)

Through a complicated series of transactions the
Mangum homestead and all of the 565 acres bought by
Hampton in 1902, has of late become public land. In 1977
the state of North Carolina through the North Carolina
State University School of Forestry acquired the property
from the Hampton heirs. Four-fifths interest in the tract
was bought outright; the remaining one-fifth interest was
condemned and acquired by the state in that way. In 1979
ownership of the property was transferred in a trade-off
arrangement, to the North Carolina Rural Rehabilitation
Corporation, a quasi-public agency which undertakes pro-
jects with the general aim of benefiting rural parts of the
state. However, the forestry school at North Carolina State
University continues to manage the property as part of the
George Watts Hill Forest, a woodland management project
in northern Durham County begun in 1929.

The Mangum family cemetery was excluded from the
property acquired by the state. That one acre, retained by
the Mangum heirs in 1902, still belongs to the Mangum
heirs today.[2]

Our group met at the Stanford Warren Library on Fayetteville
Street in Durham and proceeded by way of Route 501 North (Roxboro Road) to Rougemont. As we neared Hill Forest, we stopped
and read the historic marker about Willie P. Mangum. We also saw
the marker for Stephen B. Weeks, the historian, who married Senator Mangum's granddaughter. Proceeding to the Hill Forest Lodge,
where the students from the North Carolina State University School
of Forestry stayed, we met Mr. and Mrs. Roy Cloniger, who were
our guides. The arrangements for this expedition as well as the next
one which we would make in November 1988 were made by Professor Larry Jervis, the manager of the School of Forestry.

Again one can imagine the excitement we felt about the
prospects of walking on the same ground which John Chavis and
Senator Willie P. Mangum had walked on. Mr. and Mrs. Roy
Cloniger, keepers of the Hill Forest Lodge, first took us to see some
of the other cemeteries in Hill Forest. We saw the grave of William
Lunsford, who died in 1841; the Bowling Cemetery; and the Parrish
Cemetery, which contained only two inscribed headstones: one for
Nelson Parrish, who died as a member of the Confederate Army, and
one for Janie Smerdon Parrish, who was born in 1868 and died in
1902. There were 30 uninscribed fieldstones, representing the graves
of slaves. These wordless stones impressed on us the sad realization

that those who had given
so much of their free labor
and their lives to the development of this country
were held even in death to
be anonymous. More
research needs to be done
on the slaves of the Parrish
and Mangum families as
well as the many other
unmarked graves in the
area. These historic cemeteries should be preserved.

After leaving the Par-
rish Cemetery, we visited
the Mangum Cemetery,
which was first started in
1861. This cemetery is
located near the remains of
what used to be called Walnut Hall, the beautiful Fed-
eral-style mansion built
around 1800 and enlarged
in the 1840s. The Mangum
property consisted of over
600 acres. "The three
slavehouses in 1860 would have easily accommodated Mangum's
twelve slaves, a number that had dropped from twenty in 1850."[3]

Historic marker commemorating Willie Person Mangum on 15-501 North on the Roxboro Road.

Senator Mangum started the cemetery in 1861, when his only
son, Lieutenant William Preston Mangum of the Confederate Army,
died as a result of wounds suffered in late July 1861 in the Battle
of Manassas, the first major battle of the Civil War. According to
Hill:

> The body was shipped to Hillsborough where it was met
> by a large crowd. Willie Person Mangum, sixty-nine years
> old in 1861, waited on the porch of Walnut Hall for his
> son's remains, then chose a spot 500 yards southwest of the
> house for his final resting place. He is said to have been
> deeply affected by the loss of his son. Long in declining
> health the elder Mangum died six weeks later, on Septem-
> ber 7, 1861. He was buried alongside his son.[4]

Lieutenant Willie Preston Mangum. (North Carolina Collection, Wilson Library, University of North Carolina at Chapel Hill.)

At the Mangum 1861 cemetery, we saw the graves of Stephen Beauregard Weeks, who died in 1918; Sallie Mangum Weeks, Stephen Weeks's wife and the granddaughter of Senator Mangum; Lieutenant William Preston Mangum, who was born in 1837 and died in 1861; Sallie Preston Weeks, the daughter of Stephen and Sallie Weeks, who died around 1878[5]; Mary Sutherland Mangum, daughter of Senator Mangum, who was born in 1832 and died in 1902; the grave of Senator Willie P. Mangum, who was born in 1792 and died on September 7, 1861; Charity Alston Mangum, wife of Willie Person Mangum, who was born in 1795 and died in 1873; Sallie Alston Leach, wife of Martin Leach, who was born in 1824 and died in 1896; Anne Preston Leach, a daughter of Martin W. Leach, who was born in 1865 and died in 1942; and Martha Person Mangum, a daughter of Senator Mangum, who was born in 1828 and died in 1902.

The grave of Lieutenant William Preston Mangum was disturbed and robbed during the fall of 1983. The grave robbers "had completely excavated his remains and strewn parts of the coffin, bones, hair, and pieces of his uniform about the site. Notable about their actions was the fact that the buttons had been taken from the uniform, indicating a possible motive, though certainly no justification, for this appalling deed."[6]

After leaving the 1861 gravesite, our group raked the autumn leaves as far as a branch to see if we could discover any more graves. There were no more at this location, although the natural stones embedded beneath the leaves were very deceptive.

We then visited another cemetery in Bahamas, an adjoining village to Rougemont. This cemetery is located at Hampton Road behind a Mangum homestead which is now owned by the Whitfields.

Inscribed headstone of Senator Willie P. Mangum.

We saw the inscribed gravestones of a young girl, Deborah Ann Mangum, who died in 1842 at the age of 6 years and 9 months. There were also around 30 uninscribed graves of slaves in this cemetery. Because of the lateness of the day, we ended our search for the gravesite of John Chavis at that time, after a prayer from Rev. Benjamin Chavis emphasizing that "truth crushed to earth will rise again."

After the 1987 visit to the Mangum Estate I continued my research at the North Carolina Archives trying to discover some clue as to where an older cemetery might be located on the plantation. John Chavis died in 1838, so it is logical that he would not have been buried in the 1861 cemetery.

Suddenly, reading the letters of Willie P. Mangum again, I came across a letter to Mangum from his brother, Priestley, dated March 14, 1829, in which Priestley informs his brother that his mother died and mentions where he buried her:

> Dear Sir,
> It falls to my lot to communicate to you the mournful
> intelligence of the death of our Mother. She died on the

Inscribed headstone of Lieutenant William Preston Mangum.

morning of the 11th Inst. viz: Tuesday morning 3 or 4
o'clock. I heard of it on Tuesday about 11 o'clock & went
down from Hillsboro immediately, & there remained until
Thursday morning when the corpse was decently interred,

Inscribed headstone of Charity Alston Mangum, wife of Senator Willie P. Mangum.

at a place set apart years ago by my Father & Mother for their graves—as I understood from my Father. It is South of the *old place*, on the ridge beyond the first branch [emphasis added].[7]

The "old place" is the homesite where Mangum's father and mother lived with their children before the new house was built on the location of Walnut Hall. We had not had a chance on our previous trip to visit the site of the "old place." Now, with this letter, we had a virtual map to the location of the older cemetery.

I made arrangements with Mr. Jervis for our visit to the "old place" on November 17, 1988, and arranged for some guides. Only three members of the John Chavis Historical Society were able to go: My cousin Octavia Chavis from Alexandria, Virginia (who worked at the National Archives in Washington, D.C.); my cousin Franklin Pierce Ridley, Jr., a building contractor in Raleigh, N.C.; and I. Our guides from the North Carolina State University School of Forestry were Mr. Bret Wallingford and Mr. Mike Petruncio.

One of the two rock chimneys at the "old place" on the Willie P. Mangum estate.

It had been raining the morning we left Raleigh and Durham, but just as we entered Rougemont the rain stopped and the sun beamed brightly in the morning sky. Our guides took us to see the remains of the old homesite. We were intrigued by the two rock chimneys which still remained. Then without a compass we tried to follow the southerly course from the old place as mentioned in Priestley Mangum's letter. We went, however, in a northerly direction, up and down hills and across shallow streams of water. From the hillsides we saw foundations of houses which must have been built several hundred years ago and numerous beds of piled up rocks which appeared to be Indian burial mounds.

Finally, fatigued and disappointed, we trudged back in the direction where we had parked our cars. Suddenly Bret yelled that he had found something. He had discovered a large tombstone, one of the largest slabs that we had seen, made out of the native stone! We hurried to his side, and there we saw that someone had tried to etch on the stone the initials WM or MM. If WM, this could stand for Willie P. Mangum's father, Willie P. Mangum, Sr. If this is indeed the grave of Senator Mangum's father, then his mother, Catherine Davis Mangum, is also buried in this cemetery. His mother as noted above died in 1829 and his father died in 1837, one year before John Chavis died. Senator Mangum and his wife Charity had another daughter, Catherine Davis Mangum, who died in infancy and was, perhaps, also buried in the old graveyard with her grandparents. There is a child's grave in the cemetery.

Most remarkable in the cemetery was an uninscribed gravestone with black markings on it. All of us wondered why this stone was different from the others.

Bret Wallingford took slides of the tombstones and other sites we saw. About a month later

Picture of the large tombstone in the newly found cemetery.

Picture of the tombstone with markings of JC on it.

when Bret sent me the slides, I showed them to my daughter, Ajulo Elisabeth Othow. She showed me that the shape of the black markings was in the form of J and C. We speculated that someone had tried to mark on the stone the initials J C, representing John Chavis.

We are hopeful that this is the resting place of the remains of John Chavis. If so, further investigation should be made to substantiate the evidence and to have a fitting memorial placed there. After making this discovery, I was informed by Mr. Jervis that the NCSU School of Forestry would place flags around the newly found cemetery and that it will be protected and preserved for future cultural visitations.

Later, having located the site with the aid of a compass, Bret informed me that the newly found cemetery is indeed south of the "old place" on a ridge just as Priestley Mangum's letter had indicated. A new map of Hill Forest shows the location of the cemetery.

There have been conflicting reports as to how and where John Chavis died. There was a Mr. Walker who documented John Chavis's life through a series of excerpts from the Lexington, Orange and Roanoke presbyteries. He sent these documents to the *North Carolina Presbyterian* (Vol. XVII, No. 337, January 31, 1883). Mr. Waller states:

> [John Chavis] died some twenty-five years ago, and was buried about five or six miles from Oxford, on Williamsboro road, at the old home of his brother, Wm. Chavis. While living he was under the care of the Orange Presbytery and was held in high esteem by all who knew him.[8]

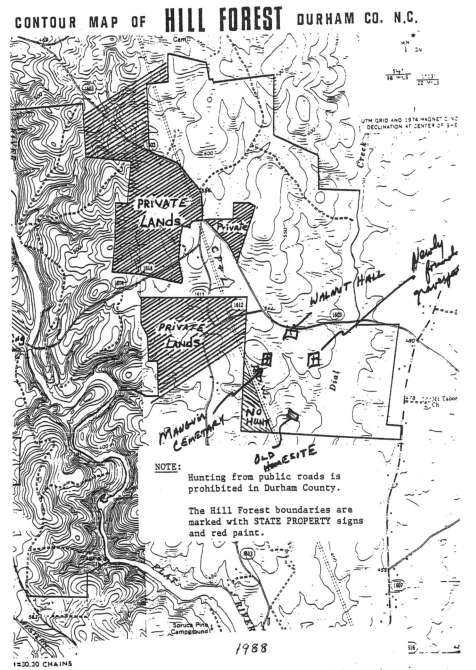

A contour map of the newly found old cemetery

Although the writer's date for John Chavis's death seems to be off, and the location of Chavis's grave does not agree with our theory, the article authenticates the connection between John Chavis and William Chavis, in keeping with the family's oral tradition and other historical records which have been presented in this study.

In a letter from J. H. Horner to Dr. Charles Phillips, dated May 14, 1883, from Oxford, N.C., Mr. Horner states:

> Chavis died in the county near the Wake line about the year 1840. Colonel Amis saw him old and feeble in 1838.
> Col. A(mis) also informs me that he left one son who is also dead.[9]

The minutes of the Orange Presbytery do not indicate when or how John Chavis died. The entry merely states: "Mr. Burwell reported that he had received $24.75 for Mr. Chavis." On October 13, 1838, the Presbytery entry notes, "Presbytery resolved to continue the support of the widow of John Chavis."

And on April 17, 1840, as quoted by F. H. Johnston:

> "Resolved that this Presbytery will cause to be paid to the widow of Jno. Chavis $40, a year during her natural life."
> Mr. John Bullock appears as the person who had the care of the widow, and was paid for her maintenance. (Minutes April 18th, 1840.)
> In 1842 Mrs. Chavis was reported as no longer in need of pecuniary aid from the Presbytery, and the case disappears finally from the records.[10]

Johnston's article makes further conclusion from the "official dates" about John Chavis:

> That he was in North Carolina probably several years (from previous to 1805 to 1809) before he became connected with Orange Presbytery....
> That when providentially debarred from the privilege of preaching, he sought to proclaim the gospel truth through the printed page.
> That he died in 1838 at an advanced age, having been comfortably provided for by the Presbytery, both he, and his widow after him, so long as there was need.

An obituary appeared in *Watchman of the South*, a newspaper from Richmond, Virginia:

> In Orange Co., N.C., on the 15th of June, Mr. John
> Chavis, a licentiate under the care of the Presbytery. He
> was a colored man, who had been brought forward by
> John Blair Smith. In his old age he was very infirm.—
> although he was not as useful, as it had been hoped he
> would be, his christian character gave comfort to his
> friends.[11]

More research needs to be done on how and where John Chavis
died. There have been rumors that he did not die a natural death.[12]

In any event, it was a great revelation and fulfillment to discover
this gravesite. To walk on the Mangum plantation along the paths
where John Chavis walked and to find what is possibly his final resting place was a heart-stirring revelation. The air over the whole plantation was very still. Only one bird could be heard in the distance.
We could hear our feet crunching the dry autumn leaves and dead
trees creaking as a warning that they would soon fall.

In African traditions children are the embodiment of the spirit
of the ancestors. So here we were returning to a place once known
and now recaptured in a moment of time. While on the Mangum
Plantation, I could imagine John Chavis walking along stony leaf-
covered paths with his Bible in his hand, and I recalled the passage
from Revelation that he quotes in his *Essay on the Doctrine of the
Extent of the Extent of the Atonement of Christ* about what St. John
envisioned on the Isle of Patmos:

> I beheld, and, lo, a great multitude which no man could
> number, of all nations, and kindreds, and people, and
> tongues, stood before the throne, and before the Lamb,
> clothed with white robes, and palms in their hands; And
> cried with a loud voice, saying, Salvation to our God which
> sitteth upon the throne, and unto the Lamb. And all the
> angels stood round about the throne, and about the elders
> and the four beasts, and fell before the throne on their
> faces, and worshipped God, Saying, Amen: Blessing, and
> glory, and wisdom, and thanksgiving, and honor, and
> power, and might, be unto our God for ever and ever.
> Amen [Revelation 7:9–12].

It is a singular coincidence that 158 years after the publication
of Chavis's *Atonement*, hundreds of thousands of black men would
hold a march in the nation's capital with the theme of atonement,
and that John Chavis's descendant, Rev. Benjamin F. Chavis, Jr.,
would organize that march!

According to the doctrine as explained in the *Atonement*, God is no respecter of the outward show of man, his race, religion, nationality, or creed, but looks on the heart of man. It was quite fitting that the Honorable Louis Farrakhan, a Muslim, would lead the march and that there were clergy from other faiths participating in the march. According to the above doctrine, all of mankind are children of God.

> And God shall wipe away all tears from their eyes; and there shall be no more death, neither sorrow nor crying, neither shall there be any more pain: for the former things are passed away. And he that sat upon the throne said, Behold, I make all things new. And he said unto me, Write: for these words are true and faithful.... He that overcometh shall inherit all things; and I will be his God, and he shall be my son [Revelation 21: 4–5, 7].

The Legacies of John Chavis

It is hoped that from this study the reader will understand the background, character, and contributions of John Chavis. His life and work indicate that his ideas and actions were based upon a profound philosophy of life. First of all, he believed that each person could succeed educationally, politically, and economically if he or she tried. In his letters to Willie P. Mangum, we see him admonishing the senator to make practical and common-sense decisions about his economic and political future. Clearly he felt that one's political and economic life should represent the actions of a fully educated person. He was concerned with the promotion of not only individual success, but the economic and political success of national government.

In fostering the belief that each person can succeed, he established a tradition in education, and he taught both white and black youth in that tradition. He believed in the integrity and learning ability of each student whether white or black. The curriculum of his Latin grammar secondary school was broad, in keeping with the tradition of his mentors, Henry Pattillo and John Witherspoon.

These are the legacies John Chavis passed down to his own students and to future generations: First, that one should develop a strong linguistic background through the study of foreign languages, classical as well as modern; second, that one should acquire the computational skills necessary to be successful in a changing business world; third, that one should acquire an understanding of geographical, social and political issues which will help in coping with the vicissitudes of the American republic and in fostering international cooperation; fourth, that education should not only develop one to enter a profession, but should also develop a disciplined and cultured individual, trained in leadership and decision making in the contemporary world; and fifth, that teaching is a lifelong task. Chavis followed up his students after they completed their studies at his school, as seen from his various letters. He was a lifetime mentor and counselor.

As a result of the standards which he upheld, certain philosophies became the norm for schools (especially black schools) and colleges that were started after the Civil War: The mottoes often emphasized the building of culture, character, service and leadership. Ideals fostered in the educational institutions were reinforced in the black churches. However, beginning during the late 1960s the moral thrust in colleges and universities turned toward civil rights and political action, and unfortunately many schools neglected to incorporate their earlier ideals into their new goals. By and large there has been a failure to show the moral and spiritual meaning of continued struggle. There is a great need in America today to revive the revolutionary link between gown, pulpit, and town. Chavis and his intellectual forebears strongly believed that there could not be an educated person without a religious background nor a religious person without education.

Maintaining the philosophy of leaders and teachers such as John Chavis has been an uphill battle. Even after the Reconstruction, even in today's society, some forces have bitterly opposed public school for "Negroes." Although John Chavis and other blacks proved that the African American can succeed and be equal with any other race in education and culture, an observer named Puryear penned the following opinion:

> The remarkable sweating capacity of the negro renders him objectionable in the cars, in the jury box, in the halls of legislature, in the crowds, that assemble on the court-green, but wonderfully fits him for his proper functions as a laborer in tobacco and rice fields and on the great cotton and sugar plantations of low latitudes.[1]

Such racist ideology would prefer African Americans as well as other minorities to be either without an education or under-educated. Puryear continues, "The boot-black is not a better boot black, but a worse one, the ditcher is not a better ditcher, but a worse one, if he can also calculate a solar eclipse or read with a critic's ken the choral odes of the Greek dramatists."[2] Such writers would like to see another form of slavery in which there would be a docile and ready work force which will satisfy the needs of the elite classes.

The legacy of John Chavis is that we must continually fight the forces of oppression and white supremacy which continually deny the humanity of blacks, other minorities, and the poor.

Chavis believed that a free society depended on an educated and morally astute leadership. The spiritual equality of all human beings is expressed most dynamically in his first and last publication, the sermon entitled *The Atonement*. It was because of the argument for equality expressed in *The Atonement* that he met vigorous opposition against publishing it. *The Atonement* attacks religious and racial intolerance. It also subtly attacks

Historic marker for John Chavis in Raleigh, North Carolina.

the compromise that had been made between the Presbyterian Old School politics and the institution of slavery. In his last years Chavis himself felt the painful sting of repression and oppression when he was denied his only means of livelihood; that is, his ability to carry on his preaching and teaching profession in the wake of repressive laws passed in the wake of the Nat Turner insurrection.

In keeping with the American Constitution, Chavis believed in (1) an educated republic; (2) a strong federal government; (3) a strong national treasury through the United States Bank; (4) strong tariff laws; (5) morality in government; (6) the accountability of the government to the will of the people, (7) fair treatment by the government of minorities such as, blacks and American Indians; and (8) the abolishment of unjust laws and procedures that brutalize people and oppress their natural rights. He also believed that although government should not be ruled by religious factions, it should be based upon moral judgment.

Fountain in the Martin Luther King Memorial Gardens in Raleigh, N.C. Rev. John Chavis is listed here among the names of other famous African Americans. The caption on the pyramidal plaque is taken from one of Dr. King's favorite biblical verses: "Until Justice rolls down like waters and Righteousness like a mighty stream" (Amos 5:34).

Chavis's legacy also includes the prophetic nature of his life and career. He proved to white America that the black race can aspire to higher education and make a positive impact upon society. As mentioned above, after the Civil War, many black schools, colleges, and universities were established.

John Chavis's descendants also have upheld the standards for which he dedicated his life. For example, there was the relative of Jordan Chavis, a cousin of John Chavis who sold him land when he first went to Raleigh to start his school. Jordan Chavis [II], became a great leader in the Methodist church and president of Bennett College for twelve years. Jordan Chavis, Jr., was a teacher and professor of music at Tennessee State University; he lived in Nashville, Tennessee, until his death in the early 1990s.

Descendant Rev. Dr. Benjamin F. Chavis, Jr., is also a minister. He is now Minister Benjamin Mohammed in the Nation of Islam. He was executive director of the United Church of Christ Commission for Racial Justice and executive director of the NAACP. Like John Chavis, he has suffered repression, including a period when he was jailed for his civil rights activities.

Many other Chavis descendants carry on their ancestor's proud legacy through education, religious activities, and service to their community.

These are the legacies of John Chavis: preacher, teacher, mentor, soldier, statesman, theologian, and American.

> Lives of great men all remind us
> We can make our lives sublime,
> and departing leave behind us
> Footprints on the sands of time.
>
> Henry Wadsworth Longfellow,
> "A Psalm of Life"

Part II

The "Letter Upon the Doctrine..." (*The Atonement*)

Introduction
(by Helen Chavis Othow)

Evidence discussed in earlier chapters suggests that during his declining years, Chavis experienced misgivings about the mounting repression in the plantocracy. He tried to live among his fellow Presbyterians, often masking his own feelings amid the growing agitation over slavery. After the Nat Turner insurrection in Southampton, Va., in 1831, laws were passed in North Carolina and other states forbidding the congregation of black people in churches and schools and certainly the leadership in those institutions. As we have seen, this repression had an acute impact upon Chavis financially, physically and spiritually.

In his appeals to the Orange Presbytery, Chavis pleaded for financial support since all sources of income had been taken away. He and his wife were becoming feeble, for he had suffered from crippling rheumatism for a great portion of his later life. Records indicate that the Presbytery gave pittances for his support. However, this was a man who had lived well and had acquired land, built houses, and transacted successful business ventures throughout his life. Now in his old age when he should have been secure, he was pressed to determine how he and his family would survive.

He took up his pen and decided to write a sermonical essay on a subject which he had pondered over for forty years, the question of salvation and how mankind could atone for sins. On April 21, 1832, he petitioned the Orange Presbytery to allow him to publish the sermon, but they refused, claiming it would not have any real interest to the reading public.[1] What an affront that must have been to Chavis, not to be given the opportunity to use the written word to express himself on a subject which was so current and vital to that day.

One must remember that there was resistance among many southern church people against the abolitionist movement even before the Nat Turner rebellion. Church people of practically all denominations supported laws opposing emancipation of slaves.[2] Therefore it was not difficult for such groups as the Orange Presbytery to forbid Chavis to publish *The Atonement*, which contained doctrines evoking the dignity of man whether bonded or free. The Presbytery's lack of support for the publication of his sermon can be seen as a symbol of the restrictions placed upon African American genius in the United States.

From the New Hope meeting of the Orange Presbytery on September 4, 1833, comes the following record:

> Mr. John Chavis, a man of color, and a licentiate under the care of this body, having forwarded to this body an essay on the Atonement which he desires the Presbytery to assist him in publishing; it was resolved that said essay be committed to Dr. McPheeters, Dr. Graham and Mr. Read. The same committee were also charged with all other matters relating to Mr. Chavis' case.[3]

On September 5 at the same meeting, the following action was taken:

> The committee on Mr. Chavis's case reported the following resolutions which were adopted, _____
> 1. That this Presbytery deems it inexpedient to do anything in relation to Mr. Chavis's proposed publication on the Atonement, inasmuch as it is a subject which has been amply discussed, and of course would not be generally interesting, and the proceeds would probably contribute nothing towards his support.
> 2. That Dr. C. L. Read be added to the Committee appointed in Mr. Chavis's case.[4]

Chavis waited his time, for even in old age he was a fighter. Four years later he published *Letter Upon the Doctrine of the Extent of the Atonement of Christ* through J. Gales and Son in Raleigh, North Carolina.

The denial of John Chavis's request to publish his book shows the limited degree of freedom which the free black man had at the time. During this period racism was being heavily entrenched even in the pulpit. The reasons for denying publication of the sermon are ironic and unjustified. First, it is difficult to see that expediency would be more important than the publication of a religious essay among religious people and by a man who had given his life for the spread of religion in a conservative environment. Second, before Chavis's exegesis of *The Atonement*, no other minister had been told that the subject had been "amply discussed." Third, it was presumptuous to say that the essay would not be generally interesting. Perhaps the essay's detractors really meant that it would not be interesting among their own religious clique, the fearful conservative clergy and their following. However, *The Atonement* appears to have been written for a wide audience. Finally, the fourth claim—that the proceeds would probably contribute nothing towards his support—is invalid, for any proceeds, however small, would certainly have contributed. This last claim appears to be a form of wish fulfillment because the clergyman who were designated to "care" for Chavis had a paternalistic attitude toward him. He was not allowed to contribute to his own support; that is, he was not given their sanction. They alone would solicit the support, and they alone would determine the kind of support he was to receive.

Close examination of Chavis's *Atonement* suggests deeper and more disturbing reasons for its rejection by the committee. *The Atonement* is really an expression of the bountifulness of God's grace as propagated by the New School of Presbyterianism. Many of the southern Presbyterians, such as those who had been given the "care" of Chavis during his final years, had reverted to the Old School of Presbyterianism over the issue of slavery. The repression of John Chavis and his publication of *The Atonement* was related to that issue.

According to Rev. Mr. Butin, pastor of the Oxford, North Carolina, Presbyterian Church and historic Nutbush Presbyterian Church, "William Tennant founded the New School. The church split and became the Old School and the New School in the 1700s." The Old School believed in following the profession of faith, that is, certain stringent rules regarding the elect, who are elected through grace. After the American Revolution, the Old and the New schools were united, but later the church was split again. The southerners adopted the doctrinal understanding of Christianity of the Old School in the 1840s, while the Northerners for the most part held to the New School doctrine of faith as being "experimental [experiential]."[5]

The issue of slavery presented a dilemma for Presbyterians as it did for other denominations. How was one to reconcile being a Christian and yet a slave holder? As the abolitionist movement intensified, Old School thinking was used to support arguments for slavery. Were slaves, for instance, unfortunate heathens who were destitute of God's grace? The Old School people believed in a double decree: God not only willed to save some people but also willed to condemn others to hell. This extreme doctrine of predestination allowed certain people to feel unworthy, guilty, and resigned to their special place in the order of things. This same doctrine could be preached to the slaves to impress upon them a sense of guilt and shame.

John Chavis's *Atonement* is diametrically opposed to the concept of grace espoused by the Old School. Upon reviewing the sermon, the specially appointed committee probably thought it was too liberal, for it pricked at the very heart of the institution many of them were involved in—the institution of slavery. Chavis's *Atonement* should also be studied as a personal revelation, an epiphany as well as a prophecy of a religious reformation to come in America. The censoring of his sermon was a form of social control. The divines of the Old School taught that religion is faith rather than revelation. Faith is interpreted as the profession of received doctrine, a form of reason.

In his sermon on "Tolerance of All Religions," Henry Pattillo writes, "To *contend earnestly for the faith* is undoubtedly the duty of *some*; but to study peace and holiness, is the great business of *all*."[6] Chavis's idea of an unlimited atonement seems to be greatly influenced by Pattillo's views on the subject, such as the following passage from Pattillo's *Sermons*:

> An error in judgment, when all honest pains for information have been taken, cannot be ranked among the vices. In such a case, guilt can have no place, for the will is not concerned. One evil word; one wicked action; one harsh censure, as they proceed from the heart, and are the choice of the will, have infinitely more of evil in them, than a mistaken judgment has. Thou who judgest, and condemnest thy brother, for unsound opinions, shalt thou escape the judgment of God? The better life of thy brother shall rise up against thee, and condemn thy better faith, that did not work by love.[7]

Chavis's main theme in *The Atonement* is that each person has the opportunity to become one of God's elect, not from compulsion but from free will and choice.

Chavis states at the beginning of *The Atonement* that it was his custom to review his sermons after preaching as he rode away from church on horseback. He wanted to make sure that he had not advanced some "false doctrine or said something improperly."[17] On one occasion he recollected an experience that followed a sermon about the fall of man and "the remedy that was provided for his recovery."

> I invited my congregation with all of the pathetic zeal of which I was capable, to come and believe on the Lord Jesus Christ, that they might be saved; that he was the only Saviour of sinners and the only way to eternal life; that unless they were regenerated and born again of the spirit, they could not enter the kingdom of heaven; yea, I felt as though I was standing on the brink of eternity and my congregation ready to be precipitated into utter destruction. After Preaching, I got upon my horse, as usual began to review my Sermon, and it was suddenly impressed upon my mind, as though some person had spoken to me; What? you believe in a limited atonement, and yet you have been inviting all mankind to believe on the Lord Jesus Christ for life and salvation! How is this? Such was the shock, that it appeared as if I rebounded from my saddle, and certain I am, from my feelings, that my whole frame must have been in tremors; and I rode on, one of the most miserable of men, and found no peace of mind until I became satisfactorily convinced that the atonement which our Saviour had made was commensurate to the spiritual wants of the WHOLE HUMAN FAMILY; that he had made possible for each individual to be saved.[8]

The above passage documents Chavis's experience with divine revelation. His sudden mature awareness of the meaning of Christ's suffering for the salvation of the whole world struck him as powerfully as Paul was struck on the way to Damascus. After drawing his conclusion, Chavis bases his entire argument not only on faith but on logic and philosophy, further showing his neoclassical educational background.

He prefaces his argument by stating that because the sin of Adam and Eve was infinite, the punishment was also infinite, involving the whole of mankind. He views God as a God of justice, not of injustice. Therefore God's will is perfect. He would not will some of mankind to everlasting perdition and others to everlasting blessedness.

As in a classical argument, Rev. Chavis reinforces his hypothesis:

> "Seek and ye shall find, knock and it shall be opened
> unto you. And the Spirit and the bride say come. And, let
> him that is athirst, come. And whosoever will, let him take
> of the water of life freely. Now it is plain that those invita-
> tions and promises are made to the whole human family
> without limitation, and whatever may be their import or
> meaning, that they are intended for and do embrace the
> spiritual wants of the whole human family individually, is a
> truth which cannot be denied or disproved.[9]

He uses as his supportive arguments references from the Bible as well as references from human circumstances. First he points out that "Jesus complained, "Ye will not come unto me that ye might have life." This statement means that *all* of mankind have disobeyed the call, and also that all may be saved. Second, all Christians who die ask Christ to save them; none ever protests that "Jesus Christ did not die for him." Third, Christ admonished his "Ministers of every nation, tongue and language: Go Ye into all the world and preach the Gospel to every creature, and he that believeth and is baptized shall be saved, and he that believeth not, shall be damned."

Chavis's thesis convinces through a series of meaningful rhetor-ical questions: "If Jesus Christ did not die to make atonement for each individual, why preach to each individual?"

> Can it possibly be believed that the Saviour would send
> his Ministers to preach to any part of the human family for
> whom he did not die, when he knew from the nature of
> their situation they could not believe on him, (for without
> the shedding of blood there could be no remission of sin)
> and to add to the awful curse of damnation upon them for
> their unbelief? The character of the Saviour, the plan of
> Redemption, reason and common sense forbid such a
> belief.[10]

Chavis agrees with Jonathan Edwards's description of man's perverted will and his freedom of choice. Humankind has the abil-ity to control human will and to live in accordance with God's will. God has foreknowledge, but he does not foreordain a person's will-ful activities:

It is plain then, God's foreordination or decree is nothing
more nor less than his foreknowledge. Rob God of his
foreknowledge, and you at once say there is no God; and
who that looks upon the works of creation, can possibly
deny the being of a God? Here I must appeal to the experience of the opposers of this doctrine themselves, that God's
foreordination or decree has no compulsion or influence
upon the actions of mankind at all.[11]

Chavis's explanation of the doctrine of the extent of the atonement
not only explains the atonement but also the extent of man's freedom.

The opposers of this doctrine raise another objection to
show its inconsistency. The say that according to this doctrine, there can be no possible use for preaching; for let a
man do what he will, he will be saved, and let him do what
he will, he will be damned, and yet we see from the explanation given of the doctrine of motives, of the freedom of
the will and the object of choice, that it is emphatically
true, that let a man do what he will, he will be saved, and
let a man do what he will, he will be damned, and it is
because he wills all his actions, and in so doing, acts freely,
willingly and from motives of gratification, and not from
motives of compulsion.[12]

Chavis further appeals to his readers not to wrap up church
doctrine in so much mystery and to do away with prejudice:

Thus we have a demonstrative evidence of the fatal and
dangerous effects of prejudice—that it blinds the mind and
forbids free and open investigation after truth. Whereas, if
the opposers of this doctrine would lay aside prejudice and
reason calmly and dispassionately, and that upon Philosophical principles, how easy it would be to determine that
there is no bugbear in the doctrine at all; but that it is perfectly consistent with the character of God and the state
and condition of all mankind.[13]

The doctrine of Predestination and Foreordination had been ter-
ribly misconstrued and used as justification for human errors, such
as slavery and all kinds of injustices. John Chavis had previously spoken very moderately about the slave questions, but now during his
personal crisis and seemingly final trial God moves him to speak

from his heart. This sermon is an attack on the prejudices of church-men and their narrow-minded intolerance. Indirectly it is also an attack upon the institution of slavery. The system of slavery is a product of man's will, not God's foreordination.

Just as certain works may be canonized by religious and liter-ary establishments, so certain works can be either destroyed or sup-pressed by these same establishments.[14] The suppression of *The Atonement* by Chavis's religious associates in the Orange Presbytery is the epitome of religious control, which he rebelled against, not violently but through this outstanding spiritual and intellectual ser-mon.

Although John Chavis was accepted in white homes as an equal and was allowed to preach to whites and blacks, he also experienced the pain of discrimination on occasions. Dr. Shaw refers to this record from the Sessional Records of the Old Providence Church near Oxford. This church was located near the section of the South-ern Railroad called Providence Station, and it is the church where John Chavis was appointed as a regular minister.

> In 1824 Mr. Chavis, a colored but educated Presbyterian preacher, then living about twenty miles' distant, proposed to supply for a year, but after coming a few Sundays and not receiving with familiar and hospitable entertainment as was desired and necessary, he discontinued his visits.
>
> Signed, Mr. James Douglass
> Clerk of Session[15]

The recorder of the session writes in the typical "selective" style of the eighteenth and nineteenth centuries. A feeling of prejudice or a desire to discriminate is often described by early religious persons as a "delicate situation." Here "familiar and hospitable entertain-ment" has the same connotation. Chavis apparently experienced prejudice and abuse as he tried to administer to his congregation. The shortness of his stay at Providence Church fully indicates that he was not willing to stay and accept racial slurs and slights from his congregation. This is an authentic record of Old Providence Church; Rev. George Crawfoot of the Grassy Creek Presbyterian Church in Stovall, North Carolina (Granville County), confirmed that the record which Dr. Shaw cites is in the record of Providence Church.[16]

Another significant feature about this record, according to Dr.

Shaw, is that it locates where John Chavis was living and perhaps where he was born, about twenty miles from Providence Church at Reavis Cross Roads.

G. W. Kittrell reports that he saw John Chavis in 1824:

> He preached at a church called Ebenezar (during the absence of Mr. Graves). He preached from Psalm 84 chapter, 11 verse....
>
> As early as 1826 he applied to Presbytery (The Rev. Dr. McPheeters) to give their views with regard to a small treatise on the Atonement. Presbytery did not advise him to publish it, but he did, and lost money by it.
>
> After Presbytery assured his support Dr. McPheeters and myself were appointed to attend his support. I went to see a relative of his, who told me that we need trouble ourselves no farther about it, that his relatives were able and willing.[17]

The above record confirms that Dr. McPheeters was the principal decision maker at the Presbytery and that John Chavis had relatives living in Granville County.

John Chavis lived a life of useful service to humanity. Even after he was forbidden to preach, he wanted to reveal his vision to the world through the publication of *The Atonement*—a vision of "all nations and kindreds and people and tongues," equal before God, worshipping God together.[18]

John Chavis was a preacher, teacher, mentor, advocate, and freedom fighter in his own way. He used his native intelligence, intellect and God-fearing spirituality to declare his convictions at a time when African Americans both slave and free were forced into a marginal and voiceless existence.

It is necessary to search for John Chavis because we should not bury our geniuses, to use the phrase from Alice Walker, who searched and found the burial place for the renowned writer Zora Neale Hurston. The idea that we should not bury our geniuses of course does not refer to physical burial, but to spiritual burial. We should not bury their memories and the contributions which they made to African American as well as to American life and history.

There is a park in Raleigh, North Carolina, which is named after Chavis but many are unaware of the contributions which he made to the religious, educational, social and political life of the nation. No, John Chavis will not be buried. We must maintain his legacy and remember one who exemplified the black genius during the dismal days of slavery; one who had the courage to stand up and be counted, to say, "I am a man made in the image of God. Within me are all possibilities."

Letter Upon the Doctrine of the Extent of the Atonement of Christ

by the Reverend Dr. John Chavis

To the Moderator of the Orange Presbytery of N. Carolina

Revd. Sir: From Reading the Minutes of the last General Assembly of the Presbyterian Church and other Religious publications, I find that the Redeemer's kingdom is advancing in an astonishing manner; and, it is my unshaken belief, that much of this glorious work may be attributed to the increasing belief, which appears to prevail, of the extent of the doctrine of the Atonement of Christ. Such a belief expands the mind of the Christian, and, in prayer, the desire of his heart grasps in one view the whole world of mankind and leaves the event to God, who hears and grants the blessing.

The time was, when I was a firm believer in a limited atonement, and I do believe, that it was God alone that convinced me of my mistake, and that, in an almost miraculous manner.

In the early part of my Ministry, after Preaching, I could nearly recollect my Sermon verbatim. And it was my usual custom, after Preaching, to review my Sermon, to see if I had not advanced some false doctrine or said something improperly.

At a certain time I preached to a large congregation, and my subject led me to treat the fall of man, and of the remedy that was provided for his recovery, and I invited my congregation with all the pathetic zeal of which I was capable, to come and believe on the Lord

Jesus Christ, that they might be saved; that he was the only Saviour of sinners and the only way to eternal life; that unless they were regenerated and born again of the spirit, they could not enter the kingdom of heaven; yea, I felt as though I was standing on the brink of eternity and my congregation ready to be precipitated into utter destruction. After Preaching, I got upon my horse, and as usual began to review my Sermon, and it was suddenly impressed upon my mind, as though some person had spoken to me: What? you believe in a limited atonement, and yet you have been inviting all mankind to believe on the Lord Jesus Christ for life and salvation! How is this? Such was the shock, that it appeared as if I rebounded from my saddle, and certain I am, from my feelings, that my whole frame must have been in a tremour; and I rode on, one of the most miserable of men, and found no peace of mind until I became satisfactorily convinced that the atonement which our Saviour had made was commensurate to the spiritual wants of the WHOLE HUMAN FAMILY; that he had made it possible for each individual to be saved.

At the door of my investigation, I met with much difficulty. I knew that if I reasoned from false premises, my conclusions would be false. To contrast the moral perfections of God with the moral law, and reason from the moral law being a transcript of God's moral perfections, did not appear to me would be conclusive. Here I was at a loss for some time, not knowing what theory to adopt to reason from, that would be conclusive. At length, it occurred to me that I must have recourse to God's natural perfections, and of these his infinity would best answer my purpose, for it appeared plain, that the sin which Adam and his posterity had committed by violating the law of an infinite God, carried in it an infinite evil; because it was committed in the violation of a law of an infinite God, and therefore required infinite satisfaction and none but an infinite God could render that satisfaction.. At this discovery my burden was removed, and I felt comforted because I conceived that I had got upon safe ground—that the Apostle had said, that Christ came to redeem those that were under the Law, to satisfy the Law and make it honorable that God might be just and justify the sinner that believeth. Then, as all Adam's posterity were under the curse of one and the same Law, all doomed to eternal destruction, it appeared evident that he could not die to satisfy the demands of that very same and express law for a part and not for the whole; that when he addressed his Father and when he expired upon the cross, and cried 'it is finished' and the veil of the temple was rent from the top to the bottom, which signified that the middle wall of partition was broken down between Jew and Gentile, that all mankind individually, might enter into the holy of holies, and have access to a throne of grace through a Redeemer and a Mediator. This laid the foundation upon which the extent of the atonement was built, and which gave authority for such free and unbounded invitations and promises, which are recorded both in the Old and New Testament. "Look unto me and be ye saved all the ends of the earth, for I am God and there is none else. Ho [Lo], every one that thirsteth, come ye to the waters, and he that hath no money come ye, buy and eat, yea come buy wine and milk without money and without price. Seek and ye shall find, knock and it shall be opened unto you. And the spirit and the bride say come. And, let him that is athirst, come. And whosoever will, let him take of the water of life freely." Now it is plain that those invitations and promises are made to the whole human family without limitation, and whatever may be their import or meaning, that they are intended for and do embrace the spiritual wants of the whole human family individually, is a truth which cannot be denied nor disproved. Let me be permitted further to remark, that if Jesus Christ did not die to make atonement for the sins of the whole human family individually, where I would ask, the propriety of complaining, 'Ye will not come unto me that ye might have life.' Of whom does he complain? Undoubtedly, both of Jew and Gentile, or in other words, of all the disobedient of the whole human family individually. Surely no person will be so presumptuous as to charge the Saviour of mankind with folly, or that he would complain without a just cause. For it must or ought to be supposed, that his complaint is founded upon his death and suffering. Permit me further to remark, that as death ever has, and ever will make the dying man tell the truth, I ask, whoever read or heard tell of any person on a death bed ascribe his lost state to God, but in every instance they ascribe it to their own disobedience? Now if Jesus Christ did not die to make atonement for the whole human family individually, would not the dying man set up a defense for himself and plead that Jesus Christ did not die for him, and therefore he could not be saved? And, as he does not set up any such defense, does it not prove plainly that he believes that Jesus Christ died for him and that he might have been saved, provided he had complied with the terms of the Gospel; and as he did not, is it not a least, a tacit confession that his damnation is just? Now as this is the experience of the dying all over the word, does it not prove that the doctrine of the extent of the atonement is true?

To put the proof of the doctrine beyond all question, permit me to state that express emphatic command and the Saviour himself to all his Ministers of every nation, tongue and language: "Go ye into all the world and preach the Gospel to every creature, and he that believeth and is baptised shall be saved, and he that believeth not, shall be damned." What language could be more explicit to prove the doctrine of the extent of the atonement which makes provision for the whole human family, individually?—-Moreover, if Jesus Christ did not die to make atonement for each individual, why preach to each individual? Can it possibly be believed that the Saviour would send his Ministers to preach to any part of the human family for whom he did not die, when he knew from the nature of their situation they could not believe on him, (for without the shedding of blood there could be no remission of sin) and to add to the awful curse of damnation upon them for their unbelief? The character of the Saviour, the plan of Redemption, reason and common sense forbid such a belief.

I might go on and quote more Scripture, and illustrate the subject more fully by familiar examples, but I think it quite unnecessary, because the language of the Saviour just quoted defies contradiction; but more of this hereafter. But notwithstanding the proof of the doctrine of the extent of the atonement appears to be so plain, explicit and unequivocal, yet another difficulty presented itself. How were all mankind individually to have the opportunity of partaking of the blessings contained in the blood of the atonement? To remove this difficulty was a matter of anxious solicitude. At length, it occurred to me that the atonement made must be one thing, and the application of it another; that there was blood enough in the Saviour to save all, and that if any were lost, it must be for the want of application; and here another difficulty presented itself. Why did not all make application? To remove this, was a matter of the utmost importance. Here I had to make a solemn pause, and to look into the broad fields of Theories, to see if I could find any of their number from which I could so reason as to make the subject plain and intelligible to all capacities.

And here I discovered that I must adopt as theories, the doctrine of motives, the freedom of the will, and the object of choice. And should I be asked, what is a motive, I answer, it is that something, whatever it may be, that excites or prompts to action; and should I be asked also, what it is that gives the will, I answer, it is the object of choice. And lest I should be charged with too much tautology, let it be understood, that whenever I may use the word motive, the freedom of the will and the object of choice is to be understood in every instance.

In my explanation, I shall pass unnoticed the ignorance of those who say they have done many things contrary to their wills, and take with me the Philosopher and the experience of mankind, as witness, to prove that no person ever did nor ever will act contrary to their will. That action which any person performs contrary to their will, is compulsory, and therefore it is not their action at all.

It cannot be readily supposed, that any person can be willing to be punished for committing a crime, though they may acknowledge that they ought to be punished; but to be heartily willing, is not a supposable case...

For instance, suppose a servant disobeys his master, who calls him to account for his disobedience, and orders him to strip himself, that he intends to chastise him for his disobedience. The servant at first hesitates, being unwilling to be chastised, but presently obeys and strips himself; and why does he do it? It must be, because he knows that his master has him completely under his power and authority, and therefore he becomes willing to obey him; and his motive is to induce his master to be merciful in his punishment. And so it is in all other cases of the actions of mankind; they have motives and objects of choice for all they do.

From this short definition of the doctrine of motives, which I believe will accord with the experience of all mankind, I hope I shall be able to give a satisfactory reason why some men are saved, and some lost.

By the death and suffering of the Saviour, a free and unbounded fountain is opened for sin and uncleanness, and all mankind, individually, are freely invited to come to this fountain and partake of its cleansing and healing influences, and be made whole from the pollution of sin; and we find that a part of mankind do obey the call and invitation, and do come and partake of the benefits of this fountain and are made whole. Ask them why they acted thus, and they will answer that it was because it pleased God by the light of his Holy Spirit, to set life and death before them; that they saw that they were wholly polluted with sin and corruption; that unless they were cleansed and made whole by the blood of Christ, they were eternally lost; that the motive of their actions was that they were willing to be saved upon the terms of the Gospel of Jesus Christ; that they had acted freely and willingly, from motives of choice, and not from compulsion.

We find that those others who have had life and death set before them by the Holy Spirit of God, had it made known to them that they were wholly polluted with sin and corruption; that they were freely invited to come to this fountain and be cleansed and made whole; but they shut their eyes, and hardened their hearts, and refused to obey the call and invitation so freely offered. Ask them why they acted thus, and they will answer that it was because they were unwilling to obey the call and invitation of the Gospel; that they had other motives of gratification, and therefore were unwilling to come; that in so doing, they had acted freely and willingly, and from motives of choice and not from compulsion

Thus we have a true and plain definition, why it is that some men are saved and some lost. This definition also makes the road which mankind travel to heaven and to hell as plain as two and two make four.

But here I saw that I should be met with the Calvinistic doctrine, or the doctrine of God's decrees; for they are built upon the Atonement of Christ.

The opposers of this doctrine say that if God did from all eternity foreordain or decree whatsoever comes to pass, then everything is unalterably fixed, and mankind cannot act otherwise than they do—-and beside, this doctrine makes God the author of sin, which cannot be admitted.

If the opposers of this doctrine understand it to mean that God as it were, put his hand upon one man and pushes him up into heaven, and upon another man, and pushes him down into hell, irresistibly, they are grossly mistaken. This would indeed be making God the author of sin, which I say with them, cannot be admitted.

Whatever the Westminster Divines meant by God's foreordination or decrees was simply this: that God did certainly foreknow from all eternity whatsoever would come to pass, but there was to be no compulsion in the case. It is plain then, God's foreordination or decree is nothing more nor less than his foreknowledge. Rob God of his foreknowledge, and you at once say there is no God; and who that looks upon the works of creation, can possibly deny the being of a God? Here I must appeal to the experience of the opposers of this doctrine themselves, that God's foreordination or decree has no compulsion or influence upon the actions of mankind at all. And here I ask them to go back to their infancy, and carefully examine all their actions, and the motives of their actions, and say whether they conscientiously believe that God's foreknowing what they did or intended to do, had compulsive influence at all upon their actions; or whether in all they ever did or intended to do, in any single instance, they first looked forward to see whether God foreknew or had any knowledge of what they were about to do, or intended to do? If not, in what does their opposition to the Calvinistic doctrine consist? For here they must acknowledge that all they ever did was done freely and willingly, and from motives of choice, however, righteously or unrighteously they might have acted; and that God's foreknowing what they would do or intended to do had no compulsion or influence upon their actions at all; therefore God is not the author of sin. Then it is plain and put beyond all contradiction, that God's foreknowledge or decree has no compulsion or influence upon the actions of mankind at all.

Witness the crucifixion of the Saviour. The Scriptures inform us that this transaction was foreordained by God from all eternity; yet Jews have ever been blamed and ever will be blamed for their conduct. And for why? Because they acted from wicked motives and that freely and willingly, and that of choice and not from compulsion, and even Judas, for the part he acted in the cruel transaction, did not pretend to set up a defense for himself that he was compelled to do what he did; so far from it, such was his conviction to the horrid deed, that he could not bear the sight of man, nor the light of the sun, and therefore hurried himself out of the world by hanging himself.

Again, the opposers of this doctrine raise another objection to show its inconsistency. They say that according to this doctrine, there can be no possible use for preaching; for let a man do what he will, he will be saved, and let him do what he will, he will be damned, and yet we see from the explanation given of the doctrine of motives, of the freedom of the will and the object of choice, that it is emphatically true, that let a man do what he will, he will be saved, and let a man do what he will, he will be damned, and it is because he wills all his actions, and in so doing, acts freely, willingly and from motives of gratification, and not from motives of compulsion.

Thus we have a demonstrative evidence of the fatal and dangerous effects of prejudice—-that it blinds the mind and forbids free and open investigation after truth. Whereas, if the opposers of this doctrine would lay aside prejudice and reason calmly and dispassionately, and that upon Philosophical principles, how easy it would be to determine that there is no bugbear in the doctrine at all; but that it is perfectly consistent with the character of God and the state and condition of all mankind.

It is plain also from the explanation given of the Calvinistic doctrine, that the faith and practice of consistent Calvinists and consistent Armenians when rightly understood are one and the same thing. Both preach and believe that man has a will to choose and refuse and that he acts accordingly. Both believe and practice that faith that works by love and purifies the heart and which is always productive of good works, by which we are to be judged at the last day; upon the whole, the only difficulty before us, is to reconcile God's decrees with moral agency, which is a secret which must be left alone for God to reveal.

Here I saw again that I should be met with the doctrine of election, which is also founded upon the atonement of Christ. If I understand the opposers of this doctrine right, they say, that the doctrine of election makes God a partial God, and therefore an unjust God. For say they, if all Adam's posterity are under the condemnatory sentence of God's righteous law and liable to eternal punishment, equally guilty and helpless and have no power or method of their own to extricate themselves, then for God to choose or elect a part to eternal life, and a part to eternal death, must undoubtedly make him a partial God, and therefore an unjust God.

To obviate this objection, I must again bring to my assistance the doctrine of motives, the freedom of the will, and the object of choice.

Upon the foundation of the doctrine of the extent of the atonement of Christ, I do believe that God did from all eternity, according to his foreknowledge and foreordination, and his eternal purpose, determine or decree to elect, raise and build up a Church and people, to love and to serve him through all succeeding generations and ages of the world; that his name should be put upon them; that they should be called his people; that they should fill all the various stations in his Church, whether Ministers, Bishops, Elders, Deacons or lay members; all for the purpose of his own glory, and for the good and prosperity of his Church and people. But how did he elect them? Contrary to their will? No. How then? Why, according to their own free will and choice, and from love to God and to his Church and people and the salvation of their own souls. Then it is plain that their election was of their own choosing according to the foreknowledge and purpose of God, (for they acted precisely as he foreknew they would do, by repentance and faith in his blood.) All of which did not proceed from compulsions at all, but from their own free will and choice. For the truth of this I must appeal to the experience of all the professors of christianity in the church at the present day, of every grade, to say whether their standing and spheres of action in the church, did not proceed from their own free will and choice, and whether, in all they ever did, in and for the church did not proceed from the motives of love to God and to his church and people? If so, where can there be any possible ground for supposing that the doctrine of election makes God a partial God, and therefore an unjust God. For it is plain and put beyond all contradiction, that from the same parity of reasoning which has already been given, that those who are lost, choose their own election of damnation. Upon the same principles of motives, the freedom of the will, and the object of choice, that instead of their choosing a life of salvation and eternal happiness, they have chosen a life of damnation and eternal misery.

It is now time for me to say to the opposers of the doctrine of God's decrees and election, that I do believe that those doctrines are perfectly consistent with the character of the sovereign Ruler and Governor of the world, and as perfectly consistent with the present fallen state and condition of the whole human family individually. For I find that it is the belief of all those who are well instructed in the fundamental doctrines of Christianity, that, after the fall of man, God was under no obligation to save a single individual of the whole human family. Then it certainly is or ought to be comforting and consoling consideration for us to know, that God has in mercy determined or decreed to elect a church and people to love and to serve him. And for that glorious purpose, laid the plan of redemption, and executed it by or through the death and suffering of his son, to give them the opportunity of being restored to their primitive state of rectitude, and to make their way to heaven and eternal happiness. And because it found that some refuse to accept of the offered mercy and are lost, then for God to be charged with partiality and injustice is language too insolent and heaven-daring for mortals to use; and all those who use it, ought to fall prostate before him, and repent of their sins and lay in the depths of humility to the end of their day. And why? Because God's ways and dealings with his creatures are merciful and full of compassion in the plan of redemption, and perfectly consistent with their present state and condition.

In a word, my opinion is this, that wherever the word election is mentioned in the New Testament, it is intended to be adapted to the various capacities of mankind, to give them to understand that there is such a thing as an election of grace to eternal life through our Lord Jesus Christ and that it is a matter of the utmost importance for them to earnestly endeavor to make use of all the means which God has ordained, or put in their power to attain to that blessed inheritance. That there is some agency in this affair, cannot be doubted; but how or by whom, or in what manner it is put into operation, or how the operation is affected is a matter not so easily to be understood. However, on the one hand, God by the enlightening influences of his holy spirit, may touch, at least, one of the cogs and put the wheel in motion, and on the other hand, when we take into consideration the faculties of the mind of man, and begin and reason from philosophical principles founded upon the Bible, and take with us the doctrine of motives, the freedom of the will and the object of choice, we are enabled to arrive at the fair conclusion, that man himself is one of the prime agents in the operation, which proves I think satisfactorily, (if I may be allowed to adopt a course of reasoning which may be called the splitting of a hair) that God ought to be charged neither with partiality nor with impartiality, neither with justice nor with injustice; for at the great day of accounts, the books are to be opened, in which the actions and transactions of the whole human family individually are recorded, and out of those books they are to be judged according to the deeds done in the body, whether they be good, or whether they be evil; and when the final sentence of the judge is pronounced, each individual will have to say Amen, either to their salvation or to their damnation, and will then and there be constrained to acknowledge that all those records were true, and proceeded from motives of gratification, and not from compulsion. This I think ends and puts the capstone upon the whole affair, from the beginning to the end, and leaves the opposers of those doctrines which I have been investigating wrapped up in a mantle of something, which I shall leave themselves to give a name. For it is plain and put beyond contradiction, that God never did nor never will compel any man to be saved, or to be damned.

But to return to the proof of the doctrine of the atonement. Perhaps it may be thought by some that I have not sufficiently established the proof of the doctrine. If so, it cannot be amiss for me to ratify it, and put a seal upon it, from the oracles of the records of the court of heaven. John, in the Isle of Patmos, informs us that, in one of his visions, "he beheld and lo a great multitude which no man could number, of all nations and kindreds and people and tongues, stood before the throne and before the Lamb, clothed with white robes, and palms in their hands, and cried with a loud voice, saying, salvation to our God which sitteth upon the throne, and unto the lamb, and all the angels stood round about the throne, and about the elders, and the four beasts fell before the throne on their faces, and worshipped God saying, Amen, blessing, and glory, and wisdom, and thanksgiving, and honor, and power, and might, be to our God, for ever and ever, Amen. And one of the Elders, answered, saying unto me, what are those which are arrayed in white robes? And whence come they? And I said unto him, sir thou knowest. And he said unto me, these are they which come out of great tribulation, and have washed their robes and made them white in the blood of the lamb, therefore are they before the throne of God, and serve him day and night in the temple. And he that sitteth upon the throne shall dwell among them. And they shall hunger no more, neither thirst any more, neither shall the sun light upon them nor any heat. For the lamb, which is in the midst of the throne; shall feed them and shall lead them unto living fountains of water, and God shall wipe away all tears from their eyes.

Now if Jesus Christ did not die to make atonement for the sins of the whole human family individually, how comes it to pass that this glorious vision should be made known to John; that he should be instructed by one of the elders of the heavenly court or church, that this great multitude, which no man could number, had come out of great tribulation and had washed their robes and made them white in the blood of the lamb. What a remarkable and striking coincidence is it, that from the days of John in the Isle of Patmos, to the present day, that wherever Jesus Christ has sent his ministers to preach the gospel to any nation, tongue, or language of people, that some of these more or less, have embraced religion, and have become humble followers of the meek and lowly Jesus, and have manifested by their manner of worship and adoration that they possessed kindred spirits with the heavenly host, and serve God day and night in the temple. What an astonishing proof of the doctrine of the extent of the atonement of Christ, and the fulfillment of the promise of the Father to the son, that "he would give him the heathen for his inheritance, and the utmost parts of the earth for his possession."

And here let me ask, does this vision of John, taken in connection with all the concurring circumstances which have taken place through all the stages of the church, put a seal upon the doctrine that cannot be broken?

And here I am constrained to ask boldly and fearlessly, who is it, in this enlightened day of the gospel, that will come forward and undertake to prove positively, absolutely and unequivocally, that

Jesus Christ did not die for the sins of the whole human family indi- vidually. So certain am I that he did, that I would ask, who it is that would not thank God for a bible? No wonder that a society should be instituted for the purpose of sending the bible to the houses of all the families throughout christendom, yea to the houses and fam- ilies of all nations of the earth, that God may be glorified and sin- ners saved.

That my letter may not be too lengthy and weary your patience too much, your revered body will readily perceive that I have pur- posely omitted to mention and to comment on a number of those scripture texts upon which the fundamental doctrines of christian- ity are founded, because I conceive that these and their practical use and application, are as familiar to you as the drops from your fingers over your wash-basins. Therefore, I shall content myself with giv- ing concise answers to a few of your questions. What is faith? It is the assent and consent of the mind: I agree that Jesus Christ is the only saviour of sinners, and I consent to take my part and lot in him and to trust to him alone for life and salvation. What is true and genuine faith? It is the faith that works by love and purifies the heart, and which is always productive of good works by which we are to be judged at the last day. What is saving faith? Saving faith has, what I shall take the liberty to call, a golden chain with three links, the holiness of God, the justice of God and the truth of God. There- fore, whosoever can freely, conscientiously and unreservedly make Peter's appeal. Lord thou knowest all things, thou knowest that I love thee, because thou art a holy God of untainted truth, may take it for granted that they have saving faith. Can this appeal be made perpetually? No it cannot. It can only be made periodically, and then only, when grace is in lively exercise in the soul.

Thus sir, you have my letter before you. It is an original child of my weak brain and I would with much humility ask your rev- erend body to cast your charitable garments over its deformities. I have written it for the purpose of letting you know some of the doc- trines, in my private and fireside conversations with my neighbors. And if I have been in an error, I know it is a duty incumbent on you to reprove me, which, I trust, I shall receive with humility and chris- tian kindness.

That God may bless you in your deliberations to promote the best interests of the Redeemer's kingdom, is the prayer of your unworthy licentiate and beneficiary.

JOHN CHAVIS

P.S. I have had the doctrine of the Atonement of Christ of God's decrees and of election, under investigation for about forty years. And although upon those subjects, I have read the writings of some of the greatest men the world has produced, yet they left those doctrines wrapped up in so much mystery that I could not be satisfied with their investigations.

Nor could I be satisfied with my own investigations, until I adopted as theories the doctrine of motives, the freedom of the will and object of choice, and for these I am indebted to Edwards on the Will. He says that the will is produced from the last dictate of the understanding, which enabled me to come to the conclusion, that it is produced from the object of choice; which, I think, will accord with the experience of every person who will carefully examine the motives of their actions. Having adopted and reasoned from these theories, those doctrines are no longer a mystery, but are as plain to me as the letters A B C, and although I said, when treating on the doctrine of the decrees, that the only difficulty was to reconcile God's decrees with moral agency, yet I do humbly conceive that by this method of reasoning that those doctrines are stripped of all mystery, and stand clothed in as brilliant colours as the shining of the sun's rays at noon-day.

To conclude my Postscript, permit me to observe, that I believe it is acknowledged on all hands that the doctrine of the Atonement and the doctrine of God's decrees, and the doctrine of election, are three of the most mysterious doctrines belonging to the fundamental doctrines of Christianity. And that there is no other method of explaining them satisfactorily, but the philosophical reasoning, and although such kind of reasoning is not so easily comprehended by common readers, yet those doctrines ought not to be left wrapped up in mystery, because of their want of comprehension. Such characters must do, as others have done, go to the school of Philosophy, for instruction, which has the Bible for its foundation.

J.C.

Early Documents of the Chavis Family

On the following pages are a number of eighteenth century documents recording much of the Chavis family history discussed in this book. These documents are maintained by the North Carolina Department of Cultural Resources, Division of Archives and History, Raleigh, N.C. They are reprinted here with the permission of the Division of Archives and History.

Top: Summons for Joshua Hunt to appear in court to testify on behalf of Asa Tyner in "a certain matter of controversy" involving plaintiff William Chavis and defedant Asa Tyner, February 8, 1775. *Bottom:* A court document of 26 April 1775 ordering the jailing of Asa Tyner, who had "confessed that he has the said Negroes in possession that William Chavis complained for."

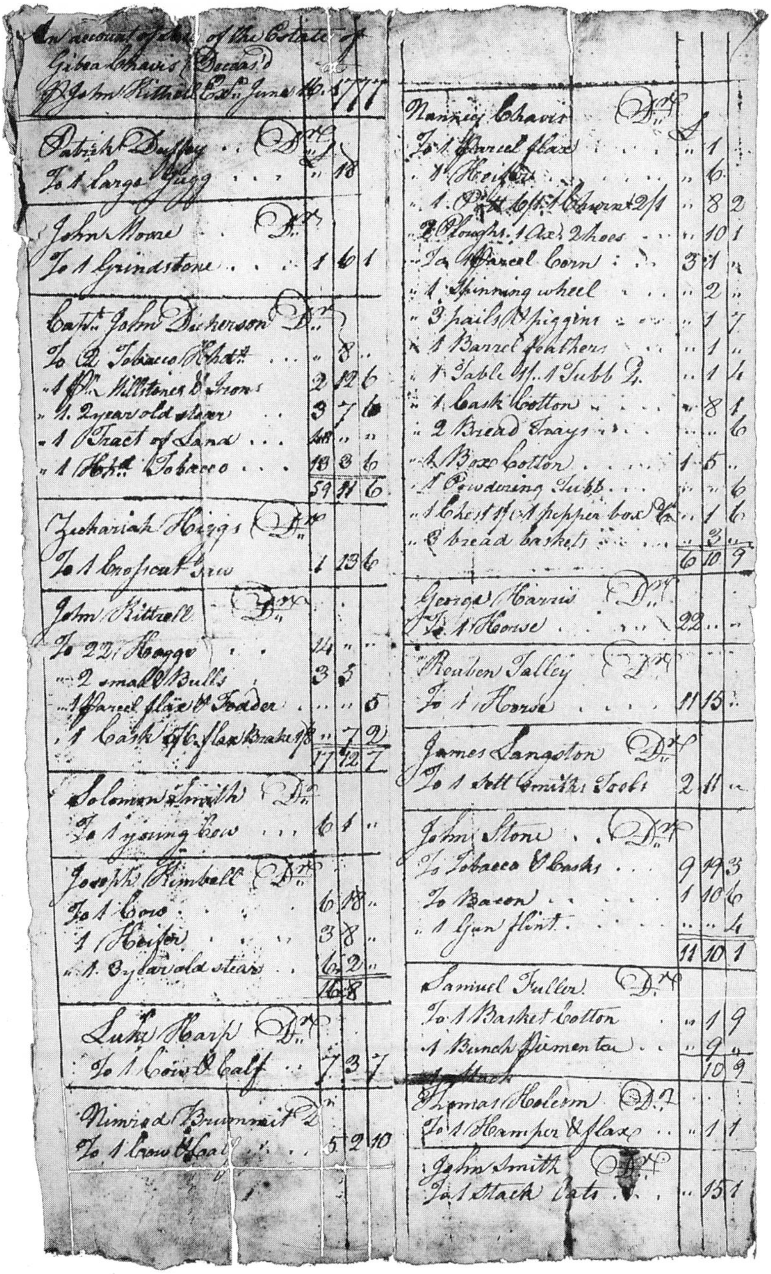

An account of sale of the Estate of Gibrea Chavis Deceased by John Kittrell Exr. June 16. 1777

	£	s	d
Patrick Duffey Dr.			
To 1 Large Jugg	..	18	
John Moore Dr.			
To 1 Grindstone	1	6	1
Captn. John Dickerson Dr.			
To Q. Tobacco	..	8	
1 pr. Millstones & Irons	2	12	6
1 2 year old steer	3	7	6
1 Tract of Land	40	..	..
1 Hhd. Tobacco	13	3	6
	59	11	6
Zachariah Higgs Dr.			
To 1 Crosscut Saw	1	13	6
John Kittrell Dr.			
To 22 Hoggs	14	..	
2 small Bulls	3	5	
1 parcel flax & Fodder	..	..	5
1 Cask & c. flax Brake	..	7	2
	17	12	7
Solomon Smith Dr.			
To 1 young Cow	6	1	..
Joseph Kimbell Dr.			
To 1 Cow	6	18	..
1 Heifer	3	8	..
1 3 year old steer	6	2	..
	16	8	
Luke Harp Dr.			
To 1 Cow & Calf	7	3	7
Nimrod Brummit Dr.			
To 1 Cow & Yearling	5	2	10

	£	s	d
Nancey Chavis Dr.			
To 1 Barrel flax	..	1	
1 Heifer	..	6	
1 Pot & c. 1 Churn 2/1	..	8	2
2 Ploughs 1 Axe 2 hoes	..	10	1
To Parcel Corn	3	1	..
1 Spinning wheel	..	2	..
3 pails & piggins	..	1	7
1 Barrel feathers	..	1	..
1 Table & c. 1 Tubb 2	..	1	4
1 Cask Cotton	..	8	1
2 Bread Trays	..	..	6
1 Box Cotton	1	5	..
1 Powdering Tubb	..	..	6
1 Chest & 1 pepper box & c.	..	1	6
3 bread baskets	..	3	..
	6	10	9
George Harris Dr.			
To 1 Horse	22	..	..
Reuben Talley Dr.			
To 1 Horse	11	15	..
James Langston Dr.			
To 1 sett Smiths Tools	2	11	..
John Stone Dr.			
To Tobacco & Casks	9	19	3
To Bacon	1	10	6
1 Gun flint	..	..	4
	11	10	1
Samuel Fuller Dr.			
To 1 Basket Cotton	..	1	9
1 Bunch Pimento	..	9	..
		10	9
Thomas Holcom Dr.			
To 1 Hamper & flax	..	1	1
John Smith Dr.			
To 1 Stack Oats	..	15	1

First page listing the sale of the estate of Gibrea Chavis, Deceased. John Kittrell was executor. The inventory is dated June 16, 1777.

The front cover of the Inventory of the Estate of Gibrea Chavis. November Court 1777.

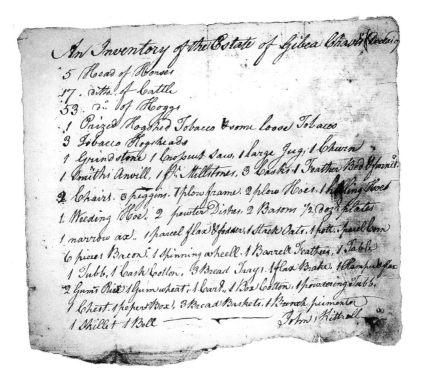

Inventory of the Estate of Gibrea Chavis, Deceased. Signed by John Kittrell.

Cover of William Chavis's deed, Chavers vs. Chavers. John Chavis's name is on the back of this deed. May 1777.

Granville County. ss. November Court A D. 1777.

Ordered that the Sheriff assign Ann Chavers Widow of Gibea Chavers her right of Dower in the tract of Land whereon the said Gibea Chavers lived, and that Reuben Searcy attend the said Sheriff as Surveyer. to com:pleat the same and that the said Searcy return a plan of the Proceedings to the next Court.

A Copy Teste.

Reuben Searcy C.C.

State of North Carolina } ss.
Granville County

To the Sheriff of Granville County Greeting, We command You to Summon Frances Chavers Relict of William Chavers dec'd Joseph Hill John Nevil, Jane Chavers William Mills. Ann Chavers. John Kittrell & Wm. Ashley Major Evans Phillip Chavers. to appear at Next Court to Answer to such things as may be enquir'd of them concerning the last Will and Testament of William Chavers dec'd.. and this they shall not omit under penalty of Ten Pounds Procla:mation money each. Witness Reuben Searcy Clerk of our said Court. the 5th Day of Feb. anno Dom 1777 — And in the first year of our Independance

Reuben Searcy C.C.

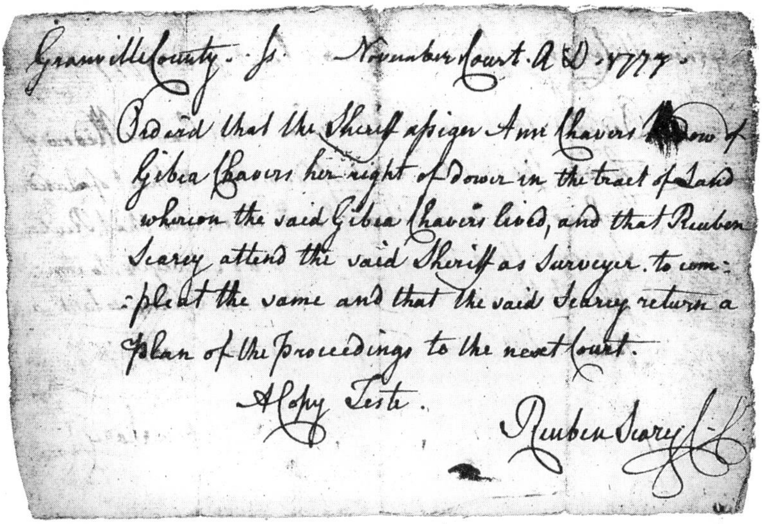

Top: Assignment of Ann Chavers [sic] her Right of Dower in the land of her deceased husband, Gibrea Chavis. (November Court 1777.) *Bottom:* Order from Reuben Searcy to summon Frances Chavers, Joseph Hill, John Nevil, Jane Chavers, William Mills, Ann Chavers, John Kittrell, William Ashley, Major Evans, and Phillip Chavis to appear next court to answer about things concerning the last will and testament of William Chavers. February 5, 1777.

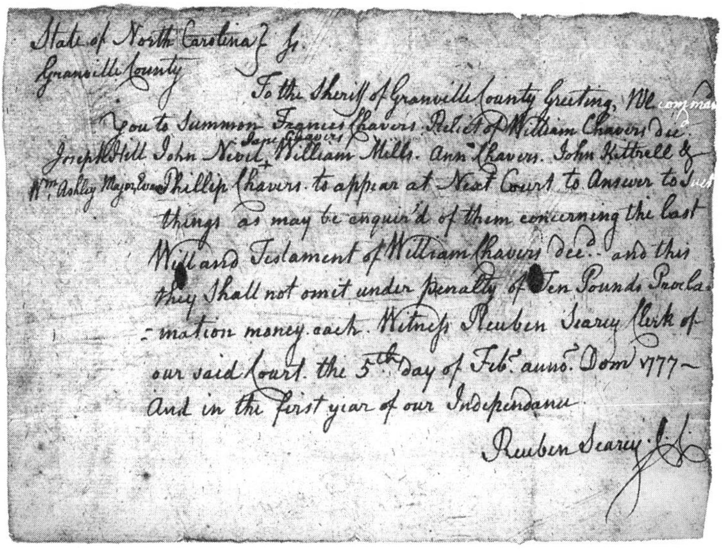

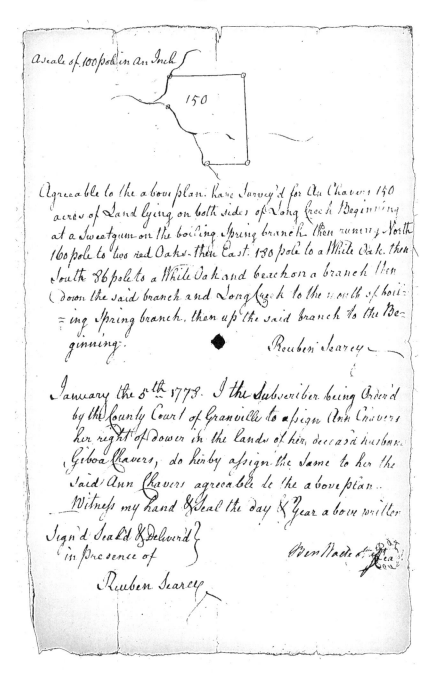

A scale of 100 pole in an Inch

150

Agreeable to the above plan. have Survey'd for An Chavers 150
acres of Land lying on both sides of Long Creek Beginning
at a Sweetgum on the boiling Spring branch. then running North
160 pole to two red Oaks. then East 180 pole to a White Oak. then
South 86 pole to a White Oak and beech on a branch then
down the said branch and Long Creek to the mouth of boil-
=ing Spring branch. then up the said branch to the Beginning.   ◆   Reuben Searcy

January the 5th 1778. I the Subscriber being Order'd
by the County Court of Granville to assign Ann Chavers
her right of dower in the lands of her deceasd husband
Giboa Chavers, do herby assign the Same to her the
said Ann Chavers agreeable to the above plan.
Witness my hand & Seal the day & Year above written
Sign'd Seal'd & Deliverd
in presence of
Reuben Searcy

Ben Wade [seal]

A land plat showing the dower of Ann Chavers (January 5, 1778).

A court document from Granville County regarding the appointment of George Priddy to serve as guardian of William Chavis, orphan of Gibrea Chavis, and to take possession of Gibrea Chavis's estate until William Chavis reached the age of 21. The document binds George Priddy (with a sum of £2000) to a promise that he will faithfully and honestly execute his duties regarding William Chavis (also referred to as "William Priddy," presumably because of George Priddy's guardianship). February 3, 1778.

three months from the date hereof to be entered on the
Records of the said Court and deliver to the said
William Priddy when and assoon as he shall arrive
at the age of twenty one Years in kind Quantity & Quality
pursuant to the Laws of this State in that case made &
provided and shall save harmless and indemnified
the said Thos. Person Esqr. from and concerning any Estate
of the said William Priddy and also shall at any time when
required by the Justices of the said Court or their Successors
Render a Just true and perfect acct. of his Guardianship
Honestly without fraud or Covin then this obligation
to be void else to remain in full force &c.

Sign'd Seal'd & Deliver'd   George [his mark] Priddy [Seal]
in Presence of   [Seal]

Pleasant _____   Thos. Banks

Continuation of document shown on previous page.

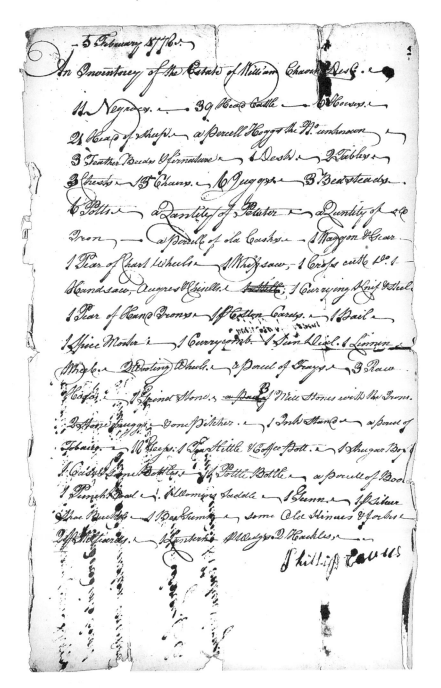

An inventory of the Estate of William Chavis, Deceased. February 5, 1778.

First page of the List of the Sales of the Estate of William Chavis, Deceased (February 1778). Phillip Chavis and Frances Chavis purchased many items and are listed many times. Asa Tyner also appears.

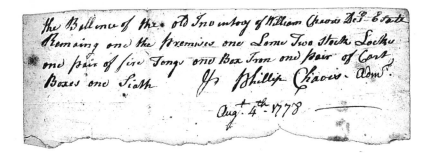

Top: A note from Phillip Chavis, administrator of the William Chavis Estate, stating the balance remaining in the estate after sale, August 4, 1778. *Bottom:* Reuben Searchy issues a call for the arrest of Phillip Chavis, son of William Chavis, upon a complaint from Asa Tyner, Phillip's brother-in-law. Phillip was made to pay five thousand pounds. (February 7, 1780.)

Another "hue and cry" by Reuben Searcy for Phillip Chavis with Asa Tyner as the plaintiff, alleging that Phillip Chavis had trespassed on his property. This time Phillip was called upon to pay five hundred thousand pounds. (November 6, 1780.)

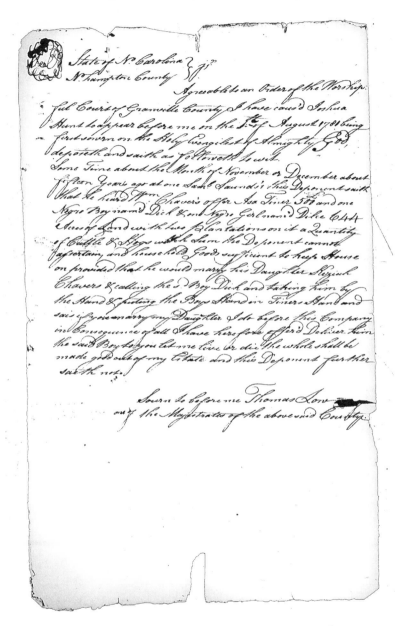

In this affidavit, Joshua Hunt appeared before Thomas Lane, the magistrate of Northampton County, and swore that fifteen years prior to 1781, William Chavis promised to give Asa Tiner two servants, £500, 644 acres of land including cattle and hogs, and "household goods sufficient to keep House on" if the latter would marry his daughter, Keziah Chavers. August 1781.

Deed from John Finch to Thomas White, dated August 17, 1785, with John Chavis's name on the back of the deed. This is the same land that Phillip Chavis had received from his father, William Chavis.

A note showing a dispute between W. Taylor and a Mr. Davis (probably Jonathan Davis) over the same land that Phillip Chavis owned and later sold to Richard Clopton (in a deed of November 23, 1811).

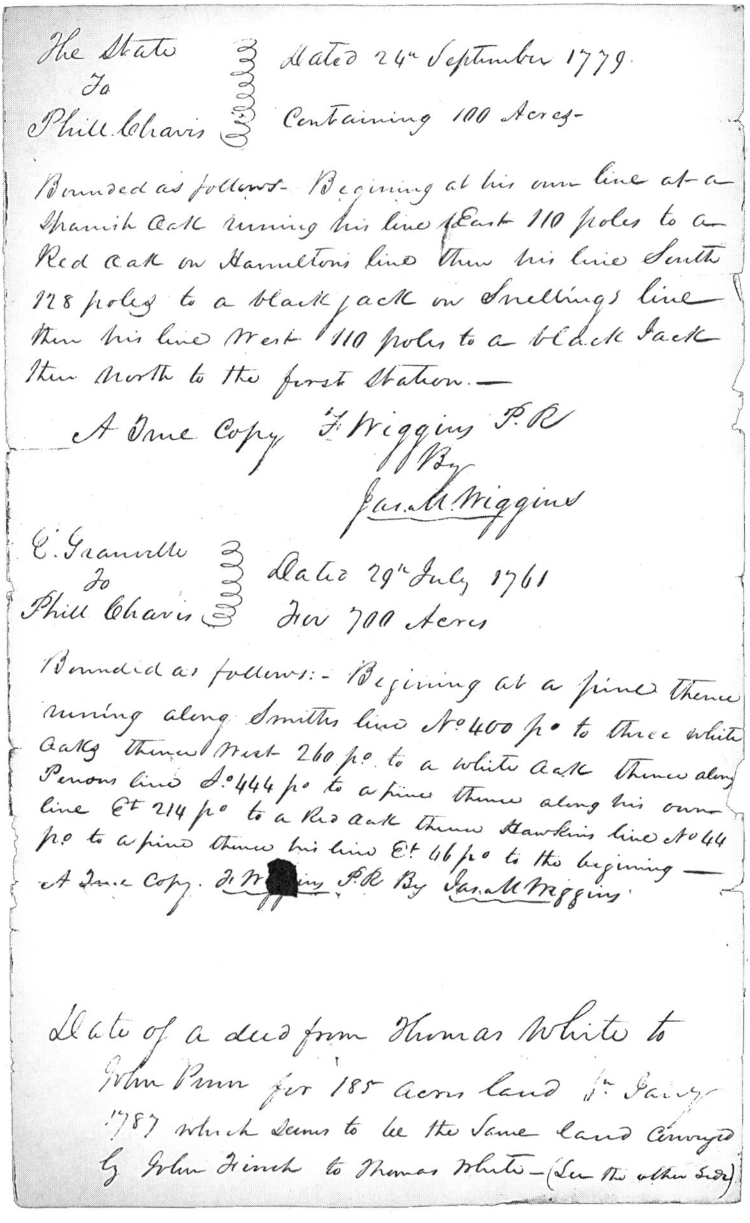

The State
To
Phill Chavis } Dated 24ᵗʰ September 1779.

Containing 100 Acres—

Bounded as follows- Begining at his own line at a
Spanish Oak running his line East 110 poles to a
Red Oak on Hamiltons line then his line South
128 poles to a black jack on Snellings line
then his line West 110 poles to a black Jack
then North to the first Station.—

A True Copy F Wiggins P.R
By
Jas M Wiggins

E. Granville
To
Phill Chavis } Dated 29ᵗʰ July, 1761

For 700 Acres

Bounded as follows:- Begining at a pine thence
running along Smiths line No 400 po to three white
Oaks thence West 260 po to a white Oak thence along
Penons line So 444 po to a pine thence along his own
line Et 214 po to a Red Oak thence Hawkins line No 44
po to a pine thence his line Et 46 po to the begining —
A True Copy. J. W—— P.R By Jas M Wiggins.

Date of a deed from Thomas White to
John Penn for 185 Acres land Jᵃ Jany
1787 which seems to be the same land conveyd
by John Finch to Thomas White—(See the other side)

Conveyances of land: first, the state of North Carolina to Phillip Chavis,
dated 26 September 1779, containing 100 acres. The second is the grant
from the Earl of Granville to Phillip Chavis, 29 July 1761, for 700 acres.
The third refers to Thomas White's selling of 180 acres of land in January
1787 to John Penn; this was the same land that had belonged to Phillip
Chavis.

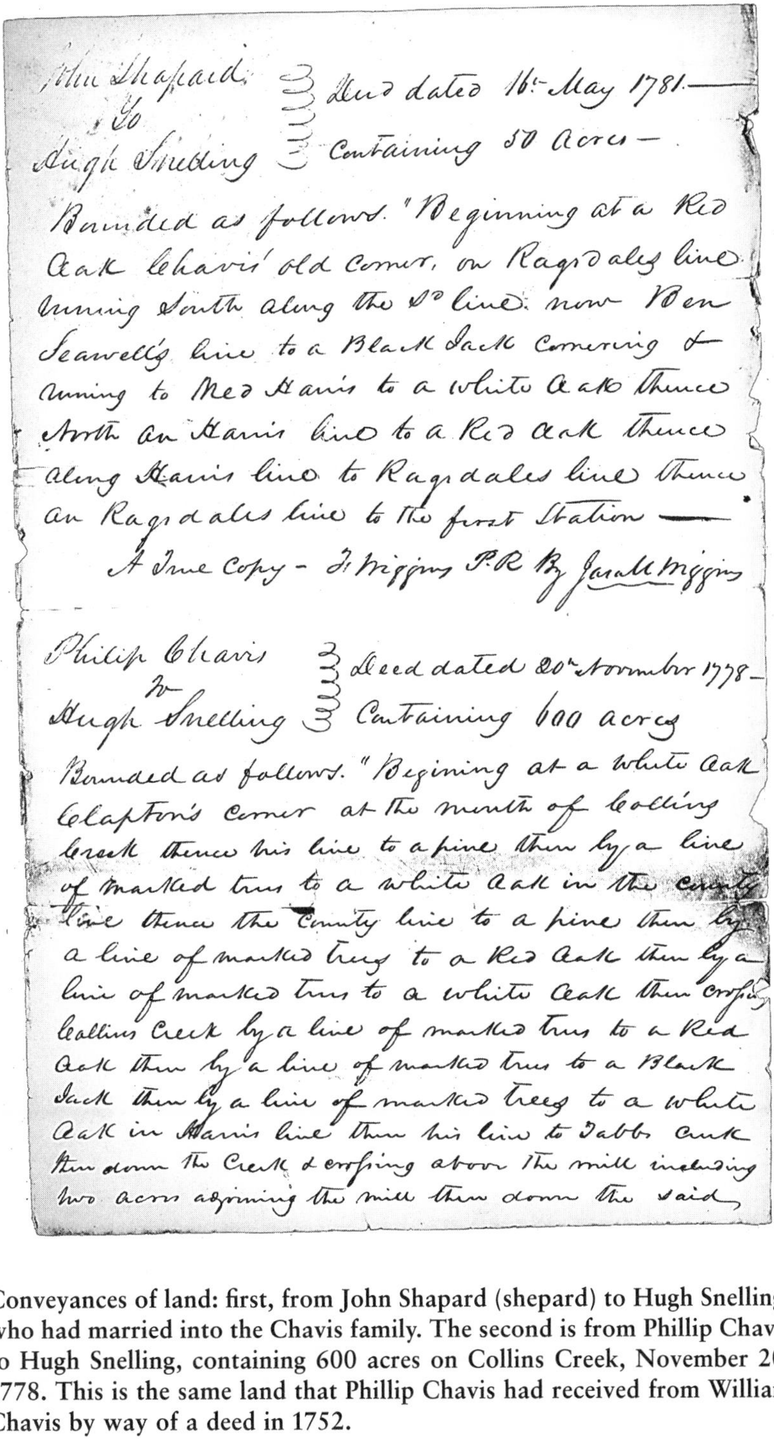

John Shapard
To
Hugh Snelling

Deed dated 16ᵗʰ May 1781 —
Containing 50 Acres —

Bounded as follows. "Beginning at a Red
Oak Chavis' old Corner, on Ragsdales line
running South along the Sᵈ line: now Ben
Seawell's line to a Black Jack Cornering &
running to Ned Harris to a White Oak thence
North on Harris line to a Red Oak thence
along Harris line to Ragsdales line thence
on Ragsdales line to the first Station ——

    A True Copy - J Wiggins P.R By Jarall Wiggins

Philip Chavis
To
Hugh Snelling

Deed dated 20ᵗʰ November 1778 —
Containing 600 acres

Bounded as follows. "Begining at a White Oak
Clapton's Corner at the mouth of Collins
Creek thence his line to a pine then by a line
of marked trees to a white Oak in the County
line thence the County line to a pine then by
a line of marked trees to a Red Oak then by a
line of marked trees to a white Oak then crossing
Collins Creek by a line of marked trees to a Red
Oak then by a line of marked trees to a Black
Jack then by a line of marked trees to a White
Oak in Harris line then his line to Tabbs Creek
then down the Creek & crossing above the mill including
two acres adjoining the mill then down the said

Conveyances of land: first, from John Shapard (shepard) to Hugh Snelling, who had married into the Chavis family. The second is from Phillip Chavis to Hugh Snelling, containing 600 acres on Collins Creek, November 20, 1778. This is the same land that Phillip Chavis had received from William Chavis by way of a deed in 1752.

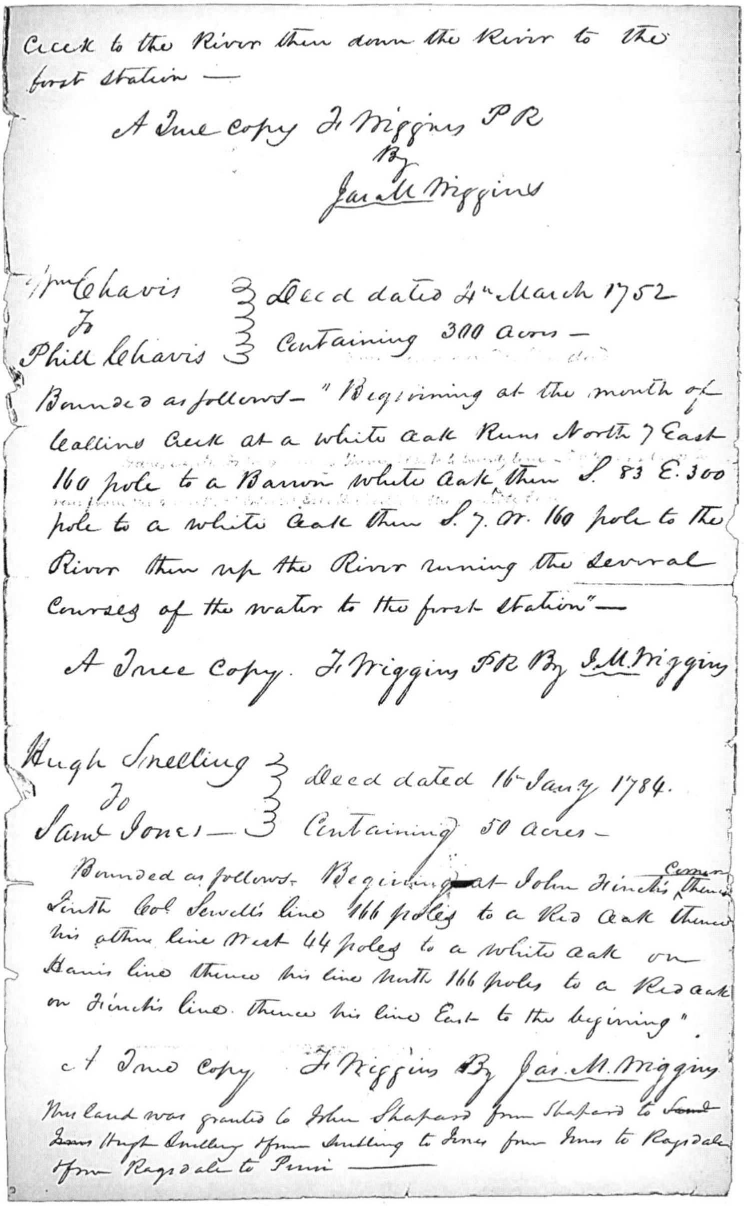

Creek to the River then down the River to the
first station —

A True copy J. Wiggins PR

By

Jacob M Wiggins

Wm Chavis ‖ Deed dated 4th March 1752
To ‖
Phill Chavis ‖ Containing 300 acres —

Bounded as follows — "Beginning at the mouth of
Collins Creek at a white oak Runs North 7 East
160 pole to a Barron white oak then S. 83 E. 300
pole to a white oak then S. 7. W. 160 pole to the
River then up the River running the several
Courses of the water to the first station" —

A True Copy. J. Wiggins PR By J. M. Wiggins

Hugh Snelling ‖ Deed dated 16 Jany 1784.
To ‖
Saml Jones — ‖ Containing 50 acres —

Bounded as follows. Beginning at John Finch's Corner then
South Col Sewell's line 166 poles to a Red Oak thence
his other line West 44 poles to a white oak on
Harris line thence his line North 166 poles to a Red oak
on Finch's line. thence his line East to the beginning".

A True Copy J. Wiggins By Jas. M. Wiggins
This land was granted to John Shepard from Shepard to
Sons Hugh Snelling from Snelling to Jones from Jones to Ragsdale
from Ragsdale to Penn —

Conveyances of land: First, from William Chavis to Phillip Chavis. The
land, which comprised 300 acres, was located on Collins Creek. The second is from Hugh Snelling to James Jones, January 16, 1784. At the bottom of the page the land is traced to a transaction from Ragsdale to John
Penn. John Penn, who lived in Granville County, was one of the signers of
the Declaration of Independence.

Deed from Philip Chavers To Richard Clopton
dated the 21st Novem... 1778
Begining in Cloptons line at a corner white Oak
and running North along Smiths line two hundred
and twenty eight poles to a hickoy in Lowels line
thence along his line West one hundred & six poles
to a pine in the county line thence along said
line South twenty four degrees west two hundred
an thirty two poles to a white oak on Snellings
line thence his line South fifty five degrees
East forty poles to a pine in Cloptons ... thence
I's ... North twenty eight poles to his corner
pine thence his line East to the first station
containing 220 acres.

Deed from Philemon Bradford and ...
& David Clopton, William Clopton, guy Clopton John
Hagood & Elizth his wife to Jonathan Davis
dated the 23rd Feby 1...
Begining at a poplar on the bank of Tar River
near the mouth of Cailings creek runing across
said creek North of East 139 poles to a pine stump
thence North 55 West 45 polls to a white oak
on the County line thence North 21
East 233 poles with the county line to a pine
stump thence east 2 poles to a pine then South
160 poles to a red oak & Safsefras then East 104 poles
to ...ed Oak & hickoy then South 68 poles to a
Wh... Oak then ... 85 East 148 poles to a
white Oak down then South 7 West 222 poles
to a pine stump standing on the bank of Tar...
then up the meanders of said River to the first St...
containing 476 acres

Conveyances of land: First, from Phillip Chavis to Richard Clopton, November 21, 1778. The second deed is a conveyance of the same land that Phillip once owner, from Philiemon Bradford and wife to David Clopton, and from William Clopton to John Hagood and his wife Elizabeth, who later deeded the land to Jonathon Davis. February 23, 1811.

APPENDIX B

Granville County's African American Soldiers in World War I

On the following pages is reproduced an article by Rev. G. C. Shaw, "Granville County in the World War: Colored Soldiers of Granville County." From the roster of soldiers included with the article, one can see that the descendants of John Chavis continued his tradition of patriotism and service to their nation.

This article originally appeared as part of *A History of the Great War* (Press of Oxford Orphanage, 1920). It is reprinted here with the permission of the *Oxford Ledger*.

Colored Soldiers of Granville County

(Contributed by Rev. G. C. Shaw)

The rapid and ominous development of events in 1914-'15 indicated to every close observer the inevitable entering of America into the European War. When the final moment came and news flashed over the country that the Rubicon had been crossed—that the patience and forbearance of our President had given way to stern action and America with her prodigious wealth and heterogenous population had declared war against Germany in the defense of World Democracy—our holy declaration, "Democracy for the World," electrified our allies, and gave to true Americans sinews of iron. The leashes of war were turned loose from North to South and from East to West. Everywhere there was simultaneous effort and preparation. Our unpreparedness but revealed our miraculous ability to get prepared in an incredibly short time. In our nervous preparation we became suspicious of all hyphenated Americans. And many of the White Americans began to wonder, what would be the attitude of the Negro in the struggle? It did not take the Negro long to allay all suspicion concerning him, for wherever he was found he proved to be loyal and patriotic. This was especially true of the colored people of Granville County; so much so that the author and publisher of this history has said he would consider it incomplete if something was not said about the colored soldiers and colored people of the county, whose patriotism and loyalty entitle them to abiding consideration.

Among all the colored soldiers of the county drafted there was not a single slacker, and of the 288 sent to camps not one was reported as having done anything unworthy of a soldier. Many of them went overseas and were on the firing-line when the armistice was signed and acquitted themselves admirably. Among them were officers ranking as high as first lieutenants.

Every organization among the Whites for work was duplicated among the Colored People. The War Savings Stamps committee traveled day and night during the drives, visiting every school district in the county and urging the people to stand by their country by giving their means and blood if necessary. As a result of these efforts the Colored People of Granville County bought more than $50,000 in War Savings Stamps and Liberty Bonds. Through their Red Cross Auxiliary they again showed their loyalty to the great cause. The women were constantly at work for the comfort of the boys who went overseas, as well as those who remained in camps on this side. They made and filled kits for the boys as they left for camp, and had one of their representatives to address each departing group urging the soldiers to so live and conduct themselves that Granville County, their State and country would always feel proud of them. How well they did this history will tell. Whatever other weakness the colored man may have, when it comes to loyalty and patriotism he is 100 per cent. true. The war taught us a good many lessons from which, if we are wise, we will profit. It revealed our moral, intellectual and physical weakness. It taught us that a great many of our citizens who have enjoyed the protection of our Flag 100 per cent. were only 50 per cent. loyal when our very existence was threatened. And it taught us too, beyond a reasonable doubt, that fleecy locks and black complexions do not differentiate true Americans.

Skins may differ, but the fires of patriotism burn in White and Black alike.

H-R-25

From A History of the Great World War. Press of Oxford Orphanage, 1920.

List of Men Inducted Into Service by Granville County Local Board [Colored]

Allen, Esquire
R 2, Oxford, N. C.
Allen, Otho
Oxford, N. C.
Allen, Sam
R 7, Oxford, N. C.
Allen, Ulysses
R 6, Oxford, N. C.
Allen, William Herman
Creedmoor, N. C.
Alston, Cornelius
R 2, Oxford, N. C.
Amis, Charlie
R 5, Oxford, N. C.
Amis, Rufus
R 5, Virgilina, Va.
Austin, Will
Hester, N. C.
Autry, Grady
West Point, Ga.
Bailey, Willie
Oxford, N. C.
Bagby, Willie
R 5, Virgilina, Va.
Banks, Henry
R 1, Franklinton, N. C.
Baskerville, Henry
Oxford, N. C.
Black, Jasper
R 4, Oxford, N. C.
Blackwell, Bennie
R 7, Oxford, N. C.
Blackwell, Francis
R 7, Oxford, N. C.
Blackwell, Willie
R 7, Oxford, N. C.
Boone, Everett
Oxford, N. C.
Boone, Royal
Tar River, N. C.
Branch, George Clayton
Oxford, N. C.
Branch, James Edward
R 7, Oxford, N. C.
Branch, Willie R.
R 7, Oxford, N. C.
Bratcher, Wiley
Creedmoor, N. C.
Bridges, Hardie
Oxford, N. C.
Bridges, John Henry H. P.
R 2, Oxford, N. C.
Bridges, Thomas
R 2, Oxford, N. C.
Bridges, Thomas W.
R 2, Oxford, N. C.
Brodie, Lemuel
R 1, Franklinton, N. C.
Brodie, Richard I.
R 2, Northside, N. C.
Brown, Robert
Durham, N. C.
Bullock, Charlie L.
Lyon, N. C.

Bullock, John
Clarksville, Va.
Bullock, Reuben, Jr.
Stem, N. C.
Bullock, Tom
Stem, N. C.
Bullock, Wm.
R 1, Creedmoor, N. C.
Bullock, Zollie
R 1, Clarksville, Va.
Burnett, Ebb
Hester, N. C.
Burnett, Fletcher
Tar River, N. C.
Burton, Junius
Oxford, N. C.
Burton, Lee O.
R 5, Oxford, N. C.
Burwell, Augustus
Oxford, N. C.
Burwell, Ernest
R 1, Franklinton, N. C.
Burwell, Nazareth
R 1, Hester, N. C.
Burwell, Sidney
Stovall, N. C.
Chavis, Benj. P. F.
R 4, Oxford, N. C.
Chavis, Jesse
R 1, Moriah, N. C.
Chavis, John A.
Oxford, N. C.
Chavis, Luther
R 4, Oxford, N. C.
Cheatham, Carnel
R 3, Oxford, N. C.
Cheatham, Dorsey
R 5, Oxford, N. C.
Clark, Robert
Oxford, N. C.
Clayton, Green
Stem, N. C.
Cook, Roy
Creedmoor, N. C.
Cooper, Chester
Oxford, N. C.
Cooper, Roy
R 5, Virgilina, Va.
Cooper, Solomon
Berea, N. C.
Cousins, General Ransom
Oxford, N. C.
Cozart, James
Creedmoor, N. C.
Cozart, James
R 2, Oxford, N. C.
Cozart, Leland S.
R 6, Oxford, N. C.
Cozart, Thomas S.
R 6, Oxford, N. C.
Cozart, Wm. H.
Creedmoor, N. C.
Crews, Ike
R 2, Kittrell

Crews, W. C. L.
Oxford, N. C.
Critcher, Percy
Stovall, N. C.
Crosby, James
Bullock, N. C.
Daniel, Archer
R 7, Oxford, N. C.
Daniel, James
R 7, Oxford, N. C.
Daniel, Nathan Bailey
R 4, Oxford, N. C.
Davis, Collie V.
Hester, N. C.
Day, Elmas
Oxford, N. C.
Downey, Jim Henry
Stem, N. C.
Downey, Lee
Stem, N. C.
Downey, Willie T.
R 2, Virgilina, Va.
Eaton, Clarence
R 2, Oxford, N. C.
Elexon, Daniel
R 2, Oxford, N. C.
Fleming, Willie
Stem, N. C.
Fuller, Freddie
R 3, Oxford, N. C.
Fuller, Otis
Kittrell, N. C.
Garner, Ernest
Creedmoor, N. C.
George, Eugene C.
Oxford, N. C.
Gooch, Joe
R 4, Oxford, N. C.
Gregory, Ward
Oxford, N. C.
Green, Eugene Gibson
Oxford, N. C.
Green, Henry
Creedmoor, N. C.
Green, James
R 2, Creedmoor, N. C.
Green, Norman
Stem, N. C.
Green, Thomas
R 1, Hester, N. C.
Green, Ulie Lee
R 1, Creedmoor, N. C.
Gregory, James E.
Oxford, N. C.
Grissom, David L.
R 2, Youngsville, N. C.
Hall, Aaron
R 4, Oxford, N. C.
Hall, Ceathis A.
R 4, Oxford, N. C.
Harris, Claude
Oxford, N. C.
Harris, John
Oxford, N. C.

GRANVILLE COUNTY IN THE WORLD WAR

Harris, Lonnie
  R 5, Oxford, N. G.
Harris, Ollie
  Oxford, N. C.
Harris, Robert
  R 1, Oxford, N. C.
Hamme, Thomas A.
  Oxford, N. C.
Harris, Willie
  Oxford, N. C.
Harris, Wm. H.
  R 6, Oxford, N. C.
Henderson, Albert
  Henderson, N. C.
Henderson, John
  R 5, Oxford, N. C.
Hester, Eli
  Oxford, N. C.
Hester, Frank
  Kittrell, N. C.
Hester, Seth H.
  R 5, Oxford, N. C.
Hicks, Clarence E.
  R 1, Creedmoor, N. C.
Hicks, John
  Stovall, N. C.
Hicks, John S.
  Oxford, N. C.
Hicks, Lee Herbert
  R 1, Creedmoor, N. C.
Hinton, Bruce
  Stem, N. C.
Horner, Andrew
  Bahama, N. C.
Horner, John
  Stem, N. C.
Howard, Al
  Oxford, N. C.
Howard, Leroy
  Oxford, N. C.
Howard, Maud
  Oxford, N. C.
Howard, Samuel
  Oxford, N. C.
Howell, Cleveland
  Tar River, N. C.
Howell, Jimmie
  R 3, Oxford, N. C.
Hunt, John
  Oxford, N. C.
Howell, John
  Oxford, N. C.
Hunt, Daniel
  R 1, Hester, N. C.
Hunt, John Anderson
  R 1, Oxford, N. C.
Jeffers, Willie
  Stem, N. C.
Jeffreys, Albert
  Tar River, N. C.
Jeffries, James Edward
  Creedmoor, N. C.
Johnson, Ed
  Stem, N. C.
Johnson, Earley
  Stem, N. C.
Johnson, Hampton
  Stovall, N. C.
Jones, Alvis
  R 7, Oxford, N. C.

Jones, Dock
  Stovall, N. C.
Jones, Elijah
  Stem, N. C.
Jones, Gus
  Oxford, N. C.
Jones, Otis
  R 1, Creedmoor, N. C.
Jones, Parham
  Oxford, N. C.
Jones, Samuel
  R 6, Oxford, N. C.
Jones, Tarry
  Oxford, N. C.
Jones, Thornton
  Virgilina, Va.
Jones, William
  Stem, N. C.
Jordon, Henry
  Oxford, N. C.
Jordan, Wm. Powell
  Oxford, N. C.
Kersey, Emmitt
  Stem, N. C.
Lewis, Frank Edward
  Spring Hope, N. C.
Lindsey, Joe H.
  R 6, Oxford, N. C.
Lunsford, Arthur Lee
  Oxford, N. C.
Lyon, Chester
  Stem, N. C.
Lyon, Cornelius
  R 1, Berea, N. C.
Lyon, Hughie
  Stem, N. C.
Lyon, Jack Carl
  Wendell, N. C.
Lyon, Graham
  Northside, N. C.
Lyon, Lee
  Northside, N. C.
Lyon, Otis
  Oxford, N. C.
Lyon, Wade
  Northside, N. C.
Lyon, Walker
  Northside, N. C.
McAden, John M.
  Oxford, N. C.
McGhee, Andrew J.
  R 3, Oxford, N. C.
McIver, Frederick
  Oxford, N. C.
Marrow, David
  Oxford, N. C.
Marrow, Haywood
  Oxford, N. C.
Marrow, Solomon
  Bullock, N. C.
Mayo, Plummer
  Oxford, N. C.
Mangum, Robert Dolphus
  R 1, Creedmoor, N. C.
Martin, Wm.
  Oxford, N. C.
Mitchell, Huly
  Lyon, N. C.
Mitchell, Jones Will
  Wendell, N. C.

Mitchell, Joseph E.
  Hester, N. C.
Mitchell, Robert
  Stem, N. C.
Mitchell, Robert Roy
  Creedmoor, N. C.
Montague, Crawford
  Oxford, N. C.
Moore, Clarence J.
  Creedmoor, N. C.
Moore, Fred
  Stem, N. C.
Moore, Ira
  Stem, N. C.
Moore, James A.
  Stem, N. C.
Morgan, Lorenzo
  Oxford, N. C.
Moss, Walter
  R 1, Creedmoor, N. C.
Newton, James
  R 6, Oxford, N. C.
Norman, John C.
  Oxford, N. C.
Norwood, Sidney
  Stem, N. C.
Nutall, Charles
  Stovall, N. C.
Nutall, Haywood
  Stovall, N. C.
Parish, Simon
  Franklinton, N. C.
Parish, Wm.
  Hester, N. C.
Parker, Alfred M.
  R 1, Franklinton, N. C.
Parker, Huly
  R 3, Oxford, N. C.
Parker, Len
  R 1, Hester, N. C.
Paschall, Willie
  Tar River, N. C.
Peace, John Henry
  R 4, Oxford, N. C.
Peace, Robert
  R 4, Oxford, N. C.
Pettiford, Charles
  Oxford, N. C.
Pettiford, Zetie
  R 2, Kittrell, N. C.
Perry, Ras
  R 1, Franklinton, N. C.
Perry, Rufus
  R 1, Franklinton, N. C.
Perry, Sam
  Franklinton, N. C.
Pool, Sam
  R 1, Virgilina, Va.
Ragland, Minoras
  Dover, N. J.
Richardson, George
  R 2, Oxford, N. C.
Richardson, Junius E.
  R 2, Oxford, N. C.
Ridley, John
  R 3, Oxford, N. C.
Rogers, Earley
  Creedmoor, N. C.
Rogers, John W.
  Stem, N. C.

GRANVILLE COUNTY IN THE WORLD WAR

Rogers, Joseph T.
  R 3, Oxford, N. C.
Rogers, Sherman
  R 3, Creedmoor, N. C.
Rogers, Walter G.
  R 2, Creedmoor, N. C.
Rolling, John
  R 2, Creedmoor, N. C.
Royster, Cornelius
  R 7, Oxford, N. C.
Royster, Frank C.
  Oxford, N. C.
Royster, Hubert
  Oxford, N. C.
Royster, Jesse
  R 5, Virgilina, Va.
Royster, McKinley
  R 7, Oxford, N. C.
Royster, Shepherd
  R 4, Oxford, N. C.
Royster, Spurgeon
  R 2, Oxford, N. C.
Royster, Thomas
  Oxford, N. C.
Sanford, James
  R 7, Oxford, N. C.
Sanford, Walter
  R 7, Oxford, N. C.
Satterwhite, James
  R 1, Hester, N. C.
Satterwhite, Jeff D.
  R 4, Oxford, N. C.
Satterfield, Wm. H.
  R 1, Berea, N. C.
Shanks, Sunny
  Hester, N. C.
Shells, Dorsey
  R 3, Oxford, N. C.
Shepherd, Marshall L.
  Oxford, N. C.
Shelton, Eddie O.
  R 3, Oxford, N. C.
Shelton, Robert O.
  Oxford, N. C.
Short, Cæsar
  Stem, N. C.
Skidmore, Thomas
  R 7, Oxford, N. C.
Smith, Allen
  R 4, Oxford, N. C.
Smith, Bowman
  Oxford, N. C.
Smith, Chacie B.
  R 5, Virgilina, Va.
Smith, Chester L.
  Oxford, N. C.
Smith, Fred Lee
  Oxford, N. C.

Smith, Jacob Esty
  R 5, Virgilina, Va.
Smith, Joe
  Hargrove, N. C.
Smith, Joseph S. P.
  R 5, Virgilina, Va.
Smith, Roy
  Oxford, N. C.
Speed, Charles
  Berea, N. C.
Suit, Benjamin
  Oxford, N. C.
Suit, Willie G.
  Stem, N. C.
Talley, James
  R 1, Franklinton, N. C.
Tanner, George
  R 6, Oxford, N. C.
Tarry, Jack
  Stovall, N. C.
Taylor, Edward
  Stovall, N. C.
Taylor, Gabriel
  Oxford, N. C.
Taylor, Gabriel
  Stovall, N. C.
Taylor, James Spurgeon
  Creedmoor, N. C.
Taylor, Lenville
  Stovall, N. C.
Taylor, Leonard A.
  Oxford, N. C.
Taylor, Lexie
  Oxford, N. C.
Taylor, Robert L.
  Oxford, N. C.
Taylor, Wm.
  Oxford, N. C.
Taylor, Wm. Henry, Jr.
  R 5, Oxford, N. C.
Taylor, Willie
  R 7, Oxford, N. C.
Teasley, Sam
  R 2, Youngsville, N. C.
Teasley, Willie
  Oxford, N. C.
Thomas, Ernest P.
  R 5, Virgilina, Va.
Thomas, Lee L.
  Oxford, N. C.
Thomasson, Lonnie
  Creedmoor, N. C.
Thorpe, Daniel
  Oxford, N. C.
Thorpe, James
  R 1, Oxford, N. C.
Thorpe, Tom
  Stem, N. C.

Throckmorton, Robert L.
  R 5, Virgilina, Va.
Tilley, Wade
  Stem, N. C.
Tinsley, Lee Andrew
  Oxford, N. C.
Turrentine, Willie L.
  Stem, N. C.
Tyler, John
  Oxford, N. C.
Tyler, Joseph Samuel
  Oxford, N. C.
Umstead, Hampton
  R 1, Nelson, V
Washington, Tom
  Stovall, N. C.
Waugh, Arthur
  Stem, N. C.
Webb, Joe
  R 7, Oxford, N. C.
Webb, John
  Stovall, N. C.
White, Nathan
  R 1, Franklinton, N. C.
White, Nelson
  R 1, Hester, N. C.
Wilkerson, Lucius
  R 2, Virgilina, Va.
Wilkerson, Stephen
  Berea, N. C.
Wilkerson, Wm. McK.
  Oxford, N. C.
Wilkins, Berry
  R 2, Virgilina, Va.
Wilkins, James Moses
  R 2, Virgilina, Va.
Williams, Percy C.
  Oxford, N. C.
Williams, Ulah
  R 7, Oxford, N. C.
Wilson, Leland
  R 7, Oxford, N. C.
Wood, Moses N.
  Berea, N. C.
Woods, Willie
  Hester, N. C.
Wright, James
  R 2, Youngsville, N. C.
Wyche, Geo. W.
  Oxford, N. C.
Young, Henry
  R 1, Oxford, N. C.
Young, Isaac
  Oxford, N. C.
Young Merriman
  R 1, Franklinton, N. C.
Young, Robert
  R 1, Franklinton, N. C.

A Gallery of Family Portraits: Some Descendants of John Chavis

Left: The Rev. Sam Chavis, founder of the Richmond, Virginia, branch of the Chavis family. (Portrait made in 1935.) *Right:* Mr. John Chavis, a descendant of the Rev. John Chavis. His father founded Dabney Road Church in South Carolina.

Left: Mrs. Susan Chavis Jacobs, ancestor of the Richmond Branch of the Chavis family.

Below: The family of Jordan Chavis, a relative of the Jordan Chavis who sold land to John Chavis when he went to Raleigh. He was president of Bennett College for twelve years and a leader in the Methodist church of the nineteenth century. Front row seated (left to right): Jordan Chavis and Mattie Carr Chavis. Standing (left to right): Roberta Chavis Johnson, Douglas Carr Chavis, Cosletta Ann Chavis Brown-Curry, and Jordan Chavis, Jr.

Above: Other descendants of John Chavis. These are the sons of Boston Chavis, Sr. They moved from Richland County near Columbia, South Carolina, in 1935 to Richmond, Virginia. That was when this picture was made. Bottom row (center): David. Second row (left to right): Horace, Joseph, Fred, and Samuel. Third row: Henry, Boston, Jr., Roland, and Frank.

Right: Major Benjamin Franklin Person Chavis, Sr. (served in World War I and was the commander of the Army Cadets at St. Augustine's College.)

Above left: June and Helen Chavis, daughters of Benjamin Franklin Chavis, Sr., and Elisabeth Ridley Chavis. *Above right:* Mrs. Elisabeth Ridley Chavis, wife of Benjamin Franklin Chavis, Sr.

Left: The family of Jordan Chavis, Jr., son of the Bennett College president. Back row: left to right, Paula James-Chavis, Jordan D. Chavis III, Sherman Haynes, Lynee Chavis-Haynes, and Kaye Chavis. Front: Katherine M. Chavis and Jordan D. Chavis, Jr.

Above left: Dr. LaRhoda Francine Chavis, M.D., daughter of Benjamin Franklin Chavis, Sr., and Elisabeth Ridley Chavis. *Above right:* Mrs. June Chavis Davenport, the first child of Benjamin Franklin Chavis, Sr., and Elisabeth Ridley Chavis. She taught science in North Carolina's Charlotte-Mecklenburg School System and was Supervisor of instruction there.

Above: The inauguration of Rev. Ben Chavis, Jr. (son of Benjamin, Sr., and Elisabeth), as executive director of the Commission for Racial Justice of the United Church of Christ. Dr. Charles Cobb, on left, was former executive director.

Right: Helen Chavis Othow, daughter of Benjamin Franklin Chavis, Sr., and Elisabeth Ridley Chavis, is the author of this study.

Notes

I. John Chavis: His Life and Legacies

1. Early Life and Family Ties

1. Barbara Parramore, "John Chavis," *Dictionary of North Carolina Biography*, Vol. I (1979), 358.

2. *Ibid.*

3. *Ibid.*

4. *Ibid.*

5. Letter from Paul Cameron to Charles Phillips, April 24, 1883, *Charles Phillips Collection*, Southern Historical Collection, Wilson Library, University of North Carolina at Chapel Hill.

6. Letter from G. W. Kittrell to Charles Phillips, May 18, 1883, *Charles Phillips Collection*, Southern Historical Collection, Wilson Library, University of North Carolina at Chapel Hill.

7. Letter from George Wortham to John H. Webb, May 14, 1883, *Charles Phillips Collection*, Southern Historical Collection, Wilson Library, University of North Carolina at Chapel Hill.

8. Joseph-Arthur de Gobineau. *Essay on the Inequality of the Human Races.* 4 vols. 1853–55.

9. Samuel T. Peace, *"Zeb's Black Baby": Vance County, North Carolina, A Short History* (Henderson, NC: 1955).

10. Letter from George Wortham to John H. Webb, May 22, 1883.

11. Letter from J. H. Horner to Dr. Charles Phillips, May 14, 1883, Southern Historical Collection, Wilson Library, University of North Carolina at Chapel Hill.

12. Letter from Dr. Kemp P. Battle to Edward Oldham, May 27, 1889, *John Chavis Papers* #2014, Southern Historical Collection, Wilson Library, University of North Carolina at Chapel Hill.

13. Granville County, *Abstracts of Wills and Estate Records, 1746–1808*, Zoe Hargett Gwynn, ed., North Carolina Division of Archives and History, Raleigh.

14. Peace, 33, and Wortham to John H. Webb, May 22, 1883.

15. Edgar W. Knight, "Notes on John Chavis," *The North Carolina Historical Review*, Vol. VII, no. 3 (July 1930); 327. W. H. Quick, *Negro Stars in All Ages of the World* (Richmond: S. B. Adkins and Co., 1898); Joseph Lacy Seawell, "Black Teacher of Southern Whites," *The New York Times Magazine* (May 18, 1929), 8.

16. Letter from John Chavis to Willie P. Mangum, March 10, 1832, *Willie P. Mangum Collection*, North Carolina Division of Archives and History, Raleigh.

17. John Spencer Bassett, *Slavery and Servitude in the Colony of North Carolina* (Baltimore: Johns Hopkins University Press, 1896).

18. Charles Lee Smith, *The History of Education in North Carolina* (Washington, DC: Government Printing Office, 1888).

19. G. C. Shaw, *John Chavis*. (Binghamton NY: Vail-Ballou, 1931).

20. Parramore, 358–359.

21. Shaw, p. 3.

22. "Census of Granville County," *North Carolina Genealogical Society Journal* XII, no. 3, 155.

23. Granville County, "Marriage Bonds," Elizabeth Hicks Hummel, ed., *Hicks History of Granville County*, Vol. I (1965), 187. Richard B. Thornton Library Genealogical Room, Oxford, North Carolina.

24. Theodore S. Babcock, *Manumission in Virginia 1782–1806*, M. A. thesis, University of Virginia, August 1974.

25. Babcock cites first census of the United States, 1790; 1782–1785, Virginia; John H. Russell, *The Free Negro in Virginia 1619–1865* (Baltimore: Johns Hopkins University Press, 1913); Robert McColley, *Slavery in Jeffersonian Virginia* (Champaign: University of Illinois Press, 1964).

26. James C. Ballagh, *A History of Slavery in Virginia* (Baltimore: Johns Hopkins University Press, 1902).

27. Theda Perdue, *Slavery and the Evolution of Cherokee Society: 1540–1866* (Knoxville: University of Tennessee Press, 1979), 10.

28. Bertie County, North Carolina, United States Census for 1790.

29. *State Census of North Carolina*, 1784–1787.

30. Granville County, *United States Census for 1790 and 1800*.

31. Perdue, 11.

32. David W. Siler, comp., *The Eastern Cherokees: A Census of the Cherokee Nation in North Carolina, Tennessee, Alabama, and Georgia in 1851* (Cottonport, Louisiana: Polyanthros, 1972).

33. Perdue, 10.

34. Peace, 6–8.

35. David Corbitt, *The Formation of North Carolina Counties* (Raleigh: North Carolina Division of Archives and History, 108–109.

36. Granville County, *Grantees 1746–1751*, Books A, B, C, E North Carolina Archives. Also see Granville County, *Grantees*, Book H, 457 North Carolina Archives, and Granville County, *Index of Grantors, 1746–1869*,

Books A, B, C, D, E, G, H, K, L, N, O, P, Q, R, T, V, and Z. See Letter C in each book wherein Chavises granted land to settlers. Richard B. Thornton Library Genealogical Room, Oxford, North Carolina.

37. Granville County, *Abstracts of Wills and Estate Records, 1746–1808*, Zoe Hargett Gwynn, ed. (North Carolina Division of Archives and History), 20, 56.

38. *Ibid.*, 56.

39. Deeds in the North Carolina Division of Archives and History, Raleigh.

40. "List of Taxables for 1762 in Granville County and Census of Granville County," *North Carolina Genealogical Society Journal* XII, no. 3 (August 1986), 155.

41. Wake County, North Carolina *Census and Tax Abstracts: 1830 and 1840*, Frances Holloway Wynne, comp., North Carolina Division of Archives and History, Raleigh.

42. Carter G. Woodson, *Free Negro Heads of Families in the United States in 1830*, North Carolina Division of Archives and History, Raleigh.

43. Mecklenburg County, Virginia, *Virginia 1830 Census Index*, Virginia Archives.

44. O. W. Blacknall, "Negro Slave Holders and Slave Owners," *The News and Observer*, Thursday, October 3, 1895, *The John Spencer Bassett Papers*, Duke University, Perkins Library Archives.

45. Peace, 32–37.

46. Blacknall.

47. Worth S. Ray, *Colonial Granville County and Its People: "Loose Leaves from the Lost Tribes of North Carolina"* (Baltimore: Genealogical, 1965).

48. *Ibid.*

49. Gibrea Chavis to William Chavis, July 1777, *North Carolina Estate Records: Granville County*, North Carolina Division of Archives and History, Raleigh.

50. Madrue Chavers-Wright, Letter to N.G. Hutchinson, Clerk of Circuit Court, Mecklenburg County, Virginia, concerning John Chavis, Princeton University Archives and Presbyterian Study Center, Montreat, North Carolina.

51. Daniel L. Boyd, *Free-Born Negro: The Life of John Chavis*, B. A. thesis, Princeton University, 1947.

52. Elizabeth Reid Murray, *Wake: Capital County of North Carolina*, Vol. I (Raleigh: Capital County, 1983).

53. Knight, 327.

54. Shaw, 3.

55. "History of Old Shiloh Church," *Presbyterian Standard*, April 25, 1906, *passim*.

56. Granville County, *North Carolina Census, 1784–1787*, transcribed by Alvaretta Kenan, Register North Carolina Division of Archives and History, Raleigh.

57. Parramore, 358.
58. Shaw, 4.

2. A Classical Education

1. G.C. Shaw, *John Chavis* (Binghamton NY: Vail-Ballou, 1931), 5.
2. Barbara Parramore, "John Chavis," *Dictionary of North Carolina Biography*, Vol. I (1979), 358.
3. *Ibid.*
4. Halifax County, North Carolina, *Inventory of Estate Records*, "A True and Perfect Inventory of all the goods and chattels ... of James Milner, Esq. Deceased," North Carolina Division of Archives and History, Raleigh.
5. Granville County, *Apprentice Bonds*, North Carolina Division of Archives and History, Raleigh.
6. Professor Downey cites Richard L. Morton, *Colonial Virginia*, I, 586–589. *Samuel Smith Downey Papers*, Duke University, Perkins Library Archives.
7. Peace, 25, cites article written by Mrs. C. L. Blackburn and published in the *Henderson Daily Dispatch* of September 18, 1931. Also see Mary Hinton Kerr, *Warren County, North Carolina, Records*, Vol. II, Abstracts of Deed Book A, 1764–1766; *Deeds of Colonial Bute County*, North Carolina Archives, n.d.
8. William H. Foote, *Historical Sketches of North Carolina* (New York: R. Carter, 1846).
9. Samuel T. Peace, *"Zeb's Black Baby": Vance County, North Carolina, A Short History* (Henderson, NC: 1955), 31–32.
10. *Samuel Smith Downey Papers*, 2. Also Foote.
11. *Samuel Smith Downey Papers*, 5.
12. *Ibid.* Cites *Colonial Records of North Carolina*, Vol. V, 1214.
13. Peace cites *Colonial Records*, Vols. VII and XX.
14. Peace, 25.
15. *Pittman Papers*, Bute County, North Carolina Archives.
16. *Ibid.*
17. Henry Pattillo, *A Geographical Catechism*, N.W. Walker, ed. (Princeton, NJ: Princeton University, Spear Theological Library; Chapel Hill: The University of North Carolina Press, 1900).
18. Pattillo, Introduction.
19. *Ibid.*
20. Pattillo, 53. Also see Bute County Committee of Safety, "Minutes 1775–1776," *Colonial Records of North Carolina*, Vol. IX, pp. 1104, 1105.
21. "Revolutionary War Service Records and Settlements," *North Carolina Genealogical Society Journal* VIII, no. 4 (November 1982), 209.

22. Records, Service Records, Revolutionary War, Adjutant General's Office, Old Records Division, National Archives, Washington. Also see *An Index of the Revolutionary Records in the Virginia Archives* compiled by Dr. H.J. Eckenrode in 1912 and 1914. John H.G. Wathney published *Historical Register of Virginians in the Revolution 1775–1783*, introduction by H.J. Eckenrode (Richmond, Virginia: Dietz, 1938). All of these documents contain records of John Chavis's service in the Revolutionary War.

23. Bounty Warrant, March 1783, North Carolina Division of Archives and History, Raleigh.

24. Granville County, *Marriages of Granville County, North Carolina 1753–1868*, Brent H. Holcomb, comp., North Carolina Division of Archives and History, Raleigh.

25. Parramore.

26. A record in the Office of History of the Presbyterian Church (USA) in Philadelphia, Pennsylvania, states that John Chavis was sent by gentlemen in Oxford (the county seat of Granville County) to Princeton University.

27. Princeton University, *Minutes of the Trustees, 1778–1796*, p. 296, Princeton University Archives, Seeley G. Mudd Library.

28. Granville County, *Abstracts of Wills and Estate Records, 1746–1808*, Zoe Hargett Gwynn, ed. (North Carolina Division of Archives and History, Raleigh), 136.

29. Charles Lee Smith, *The History of Education in North Carolina* (Washington, DC: Government Printing Office, 1888), 138–141.

30. Guion Griffin Johnson, *Ante-bellum North Carolina* (Chapel Hill: University of North Carolina Press, 1937), 189–191.

31. John Spencer Bassett, *Slavery and Servitude in the Colony of North Carolina* (Baltimore: Johns Hopkins University Press, 1896), 737.

32. Stephen B. Weeks, "John Chavis, Ante-bellum Negro," *The Southern Workman* (Feb. 1914), 101–106.

33. Daniel L. Boyd, *Free-Born Negro: The Life of John Chavis*, B.A. thesis, Princeton University, 1947, 221.

34. Edgar W. Knight, *The Academy Movement in the South*, n.p., n.d.; and Edgar W. Knight, "Notes on John Chavis," *The North Carolina Historical Review* VII, no. 3 (July 1930).

35. Shaw.

36. Carter G. Woodson, *The Education of the Negro Prior to 1861*, 2nd ed. (Washington, DC: Association for the Study of Negro Life and History, 1919), 181–182.

37. Knight, "Notes on John Chavis."

38. *The Princeton Book* (Boston: Houghton, Osgood and Company; Cambridge: Riverside, 1879).

39. Varnum L. Collins, *President Witherspoon: A Biography* (Princeton, NJ: Princeton University Press, 1928), 206.

40. *Ibid.*, 196.
41. *Ibid.*, 197.
42. *The Princeton Book*, 130.
43. Collins, 224.
44. *Ibid.*
45. Rockbridge County, Virginia, *Rockbridge County Court Order Book #6*, 10.

3. Chavis's Christian Ministry

1. John Chavis, *Letter Upon the Doctrine of the Extent of the Atonement of Christ* (Raleigh: J. Gales & Son, 1837), 4, 13.
2. Marcus W. Jernigan, "Slavery and Conversion in the American Colonies," *American Historical Review* 21, 504.
3. *Ibid.*, 505.
4. *Ibid.*, 506.
5. *Ibid.* Jernigan quotes from the *Archives of Maryland*, Vol. I, 256, 533.
6. *Ibid.* Jernigan quotes Hening, *Statutes of Virginia*, Vol. II, 260.
7. *Ibid.*, 507.
8. *Ibid.*, 511.
9. *Ibid.* Jernigan cites Humphreys, *An Historical Account of the S. P. G.*, 250–270.
10. *Ibid.*, 512.
11. *Ibid.*, 519.
12. *Ibid.*, 523.
13. *Ibid.*, 524. Jernigan quotes from *An Abstract of the S. P. G., 1757–1758*, 50.
14. *Ibid.*, 529, Jernigan quotes from *An Abstract of the S. P. G., 1725–1726*, 37–38.
15. Ernest Trice Thompson, *Presbyterians in the South, Vol. I; 1607–1861* (Richmond VA: John Knox, 1963), 189.
16. *Ibid.*, 195.
17. *Ibid.*
18. *Minutes of the Lexington Presbytery*, October 19, 1799, Vol. III, 158, Presbyterian Study Center, Montreat, North Carolina.
19. *Minutes of the Lexington Presbytery*, October 23, 1800–October 25, 1800, Presbyterian Study Center, Montreat, North Carolina.
20. *Minutes of the Lexington Presbytery*, November 18–19, 1800, Presbyterian Study Center, Montreat, North Carolina.
21. *Ibid.*
22. *Ibid.*
23. *Presbyterian General Assembly Minutes: Excerpts from Minutes*

of the Standing Committee of Missions of the Presbyterian Church May 21, 1803, Presbyterian Historical Society, Philadelphia.

24. Minutes of the Lexington Presbytery June 9, 1801, Presbyterian Study Center, Montreat, North Carolina.

25. *Ibid.*

26. *Ibid.*

27. Thompson, 189.

28. Letter from Chavis to Mangum, September 3, 1831. Willie P. Mangum Collection.

29. Letter from Chavis to Mangum, September 3, 1831. Also see letter from Joseph B. Hinton to John Gray Blount, Raleigh, N.C., Dec. 23, 1830, in *The John Gray Blount Papers*, Vol. IV, 1803–1833, ed. David T. Morgan (Raleigh: N.C. Archives and History, 1982). Rebellions by slaves, however, did not begin in the nineteenth century. A case is recorded on April 19, 1794, of a slave named Quillo in Granville County, North Carolina, who wanted to organize his fellow slaves to hold a rebellion. See *Granville County Court Record*, sworn affidavit by James Hunt, April 19, 1794.

30. Edgar W. Knight, "Notes on John Chavis," *The North Carolina Historical Review* VII, no. 3 (July 1930), 336.

31. F. H. Johnston, "Excerpts from the Orange Presbytery," *North Carolina Presbyterian*, 1883.

32. *Ibid.*

4. A Trailblazer in the Teaching Profession

1. Letter from John Chavis to Willie P. Mangum, March 10, 1832, *Willie P. Mangum Collection,* North Carolina Division of Archives and History, Raleigh.

2. Barbara Parramore, "John Chavis," *Dictionary of North Carolina Biography,* Vol. I (1979), 358.

3. See references to mixed Presbyterian congregations in W. H. Gregory, "History of Old Shiloh Presbyterian Church," *Presbyterian Standard* (April, 11, 1906).

4. Charles Lee Smith, *The History of Education in North Carolina* (Washington, DC: Government Printing Office, 1888).

5. *Ibid.*, 139.

6. Personal interview.

7. Elizabeth Reid Murray, *Wake: Capital County of North Carolina,* Vol. I (Raleigh: Capital County, 1983), 188. Sidney Kaplan, *The Black Presence in the Era of the American Revolution, 1770–1800* (Washington: National Portrait Gallery, Smithsonian Institution, 1973), 100.

8. John Chavis School," advertisement in the *Raleigh Register*, Thursday, August 26, 1808. Also see Charles L. Coon, *North Carolina Schools*

and Academies: A Documentary History (Raleigh: Edwards and Broughton, 1915), 515.

   9. Kaplan, 101.

   10. G. C. Shaw, *John Chavis* (Binghamton, N.Y.: Vail-Ballou, 1931), 25.

   11. Murray, 189.

   12. Personal Interview.

   13. Murray cites Shaw, 21–22. Also see *The Raleigh Register*, cited in note 8.

   14. Smith, 140.

   15. *Ibid.*

   16. Edgar W. Knight, "Notes on John Chavis," *The North Carolina Historical Review* VII, no. 3 (July 1930), 339.

   17. Shaw, 3–6, 22.

   18. Letter from John Chavis to Willie P. Mangum, September 3, 1831, *Willie P. Mangum Collection*, North Carolina Division of Archives and History, Raleigh.

   19. Lindley Murray, *English Grammar: Adapted to the Different Classes of Learners* (Newark, New Jersey: Benjamin Olds, 1834), 5.

   20. *Ibid.*, 6.

   21. *Ibid.*

   22. Henry Pattillo, *A Geographical Catechism*, N.W. Walker, ed. (Princeton NJ: Princeton University, Spear Theological Library; also Chapel Hill: University of North Carolina Press, 1900).

   23. C. H. Mebane, "Report on John Chavis from Superintendent of Public Instruction of North Carolina from 1896–98." W. H. Ruffner, handwritten "Notes on John Chavis," Presbyterian Study Center, Montreat, North Carolina.

5. Mentor, Confidant, and Astute Business Man

   1. Letter from John Chavis to John Haywood, October 1817, *John Chavis Papers*, Southern Historical Collection, Wilson Library, University of North Carolina at Chapel Hill.

   2. Letter from John Chavis to John Haywood, July 3, 1822, *Willie P. Mangum Collection*, North Carolina Division of Archives and History, Raleigh.

   3. Letter from John Chavis to Willie P. Mangum, January 28, 1825, *Willie P. Mangum Collection*, North Carolina Division of Archives and History, Raleigh.

   4. Letter from John Chavis to Paul Cameron, July 1, 1825, Duke University, Perkins Library Archives.

   5. *Ibid.*

   6. Letter from John Chavis to Willie P. Mangum, November 20, 1825,

Willie P. Mangum Collection, North Carolina Division of Archives and History, Raleigh.

7. Letter from John Chavis to Willie P. Mangum, November 16, 1827, *Willie P. Mangum Collection*, North Carolina Division of Archives and History, Raleigh.

8. Letter from John Chavis to Willie P. Mangum, March 11, 1828, *Willie P. Mangum Collection*, North Carolina Division of Archives and History, Raleigh.

9. *Ibid.*

10. Indenture, W. P. Mangum to James Webb and Thomas D. Watts, April 25, 1828. *Willie P. Mangum Collection*. North Carolina Archives.

11. Warrant Robert Cozart vs. Willie P. Mangum and Walter A. Mangum, April 26, 1828.

12. Letter from W. M. Green to Willie P. Mangum, March 12, 1829, *Willie P. Mangum Collection*, North Carolina Division of Archives and History, Raleigh.

13. Letter from Chavis to Mangum, September 3, 1831, *Willie P. Mangum Collection*, North Carolina Division of Archives and History, Raleigh.

14. *Ibid.*

15. *Ibid.*

16. *Ibid.*

17. Letter from Willie P. Mangum to Charity A. Mangum, February 18, 1832. *Willie P. Mangum Collection*, North Carolina Division of Archives and History, Raleigh.

18. Letter from John Chavis to Willie P. Mangum, March 10, 1832. *Willie P. Mangum Collection*, North Carolina Division of Archives and History, Raleigh.

19. *Ibid.*

20. Letter from John Chavis to Willie P. Mangum, July 21, 1832, *Willie P. Mangum Collection*, North Carolina Division of Archives and History, Raleigh.

21. *Ibid.*

22. Letter from John Chavis to Willie P. Mangum, August 8, 1832, *Willie P. Mangum Collection*, North Carolina Division of Archives and History, Raleigh.

23. *Ibid.*

24. Letter from John Chavis to Willie P. Mangum, October 1, 1832, *Willie P. Mangum Collection*, North Carolina Division of Archives and History, Raleigh.

25. Letter from John Chavis to Willie P. Mangum, November 3, 1832, *Willie P. Mangum Collection*, North Carolina Division of Archives and History, Raleigh.

26. *Ibid.*

27. Letter from Willie P. Mangum to Charity Mangum, December 15,

1832, *Willie P. Mangum Collection*, North Carolina Division of Archives and History, Raleigh.

28. Letter from John Chavis to Willie P. Mangum, February 26, 1834, *Willie P. Mangum Collection*, North Carolina Division of Archives and History, Raleigh.

29. Henry Thomas Shanks, ed., *The Papers of Willie Person Mangum*, Vol. II, 1833–1838 (Raleigh: State Department of Archives and History, 1952), 104.

30. Letter from John Chavis to Willie P. Mangum, February 26, 1834.

31. Wake County, *Real Estate Conveyances 1800–1805*, North Carolina Division of Archives and History, Raleigh.

32. Wake County, *Real Estate Conveyances 1806–1807*, North Carolina Division of Archives and History, Raleigh.

33. Wake County, *Real Estate Conveyances* 1811 and 1813, North Carolina Division of Archives and History, Raleigh.

34. Wake County, *Real Estate Conveyances*, 1815.

35. Wake County, Deed, John Chavis to William E. Roberts and William Holloway, 1822, Wake County Register of Deeds.

36. Wake County, Deed, Gatsey Mitchell and Alfred Mitchell to William Chavis, heirs, July 5, 1870, *Wake County Register of Deeds*, Book 31, 354, pages 529–531.

37. See Alfred Mitchell and Gatsey Mitchell to John Chavors (sic), Lizzie Austin, and Sallie Chavers, *Wake County Deeds*, 1870, pages 529–531; Andrew Syme et al. to Sarah Walker, *Wake County Deeds*, 1873, pages 184–186; Sarah Walker et al. to A.B. Hunter, Treas., St. Augustine's Normal School, *Wake County Deeds*, 1914, pages 348–349; and Affidavit, Sarah Walker & Hus. Collins Walker, Hannah Jones & Hus. Ernest Johns to Saint Augustine's School, 1930, *Wake County Deeds*. Sarah Walker was the daughter of Gatsey Mitchell.

38. Interview with Mrs. Asa Turner of Raleigh in 1988.

39. Granville County, "Marriage Bonds," Elizabeth Hicks Hummel, ed., *Hicks' History of Granville County*, Vol. I (1965), Richard B. Thornton Library Genealogical Room, Oxford, North Carolina.

40. *Ibid.*

41. Granville County, "List of Taxables for 1762 in Granville County and Census of Granville County," *North Carolina Genealogical Society Journal* XII, No. 3 (August 1986), 155.

6. Saga of the Chavis Family

1. Granville County, *Index of Grantors, 1746–1869*, Books A, B, C, D, E, G, H, K, L, N, O, P, Q, R, T, V, and Z. Letter C in each book indicates where the Chavises granted land to settlers. Richard B. Thornton Library Genealogical Room, Oxford, North Carolina.

2. *North Carolina Genealogical Society Journal*, February 1985, p. 44.

3. Brent Howard Holcomb, ed., *Bute County, North Carolina, Minutes of the Court of Pleas and Quarter Sessions 1767–1779* (Raleigh: State Library of North Carolina, 1988), 77–78.

4. Holcomb, minutes of 15 November 1771, page 204, and also Minutes of February 1772, page 215.

5. Robert Diggs Wimberly Connor. "The Granville District," in *North Carolina: Rebuilding an Ancient Commonwealth 1585–1925*, Vol. I (New York: The American Historical Society, 1929), 231.

7. A Path of Fire

1. "Washington and Lee University: A Natural Historic Landmark" (Richmond: Virginia State Library, 1973).

2. Varnum L. Collins, *President Witherspoon: A Biography* (Princeton NJ: Princeton University Press, 1928).

3. Carter G. Woodson, *Negro Makers of History*, 5th ed. (Washington: Associated Publishers, 1968).

4. Gossie H. Hudson, "John Chavis, 1763–1838: A Social-Psychological Study," *The Journal of Negro History* LXIV, no. 2 (Spring 1979), 142–156.

5. *Ibid.*, 149.

6. Letter from John Chavis to Willie P. Mangum, November 3, 1832, *Willie P. Mangum Collection*, North Carolina Division of Archives and History, Raleigh.

7. Letter from John Chavis to Willie P. Mangum, August 8, 1832, *Willie P. Mangum Collection*, North Carolina Division of Archives and History, Raleigh.

8. W.H. Ruffner, handwritten "Notes on John Chavis," Presbyterian Study Center, Montreat, North Carolina.

9. Edgar Knight, "Notes on John Chavis," *The North Carolina Historical Review* VII no. 3 (July 1930), 340.

10. Ruffner.

11. Letter from John Chavis to Willie P. Mangum, February 1, 1837, *Willie P. Mangum*, North Carolina Division of Archives and History, Raleigh.

8. Resurrection: In Search of His Gravesite

1. G. C. Shaw, *John Chavis* (Binghamton, N.Y.: Vail-Ballou Press, 1931), viii.

2. Michael Hill, "Historical Research Report: The Mangum Family Cemetery, Durham, North Carolina," January 4, 1984, 14–15, North Carolina Archives. Hill quotes *Durham County Deed Book 10, 19,* p. 742. Interview with Larry Jervis of the School of Forestry of North Carolina State University, December 12, 1983.

3. Hill, 5.

4. Hill, 10, cites a biographical sketch of Willie P. Mangum, written by William A. Graham in the *Hillsborough Recorder,* September 11, 1861, and reprinted in the *Raleigh Register,* September 18, 1861.

5. Hill, 13.

6. *Ibid.,* 1.

7. Letter from Priestley H. Mangum to Willie P. Mangum, March 14, 1829, *Willie P. Mangum Collection,* North Carolina Division of Archives and History, Raleigh.

8. [Name unknown] Walker, "John Chavis" *The North Carolina Presbyterian* XVII, no. 337 (January 31, 1883), Presbyterian Study Center, Montreat, North Carolina.

9. Letter from J. H. Horner to Dr. Charles Phillips, May 14, 1883, Southern Historical Collection, Wilson Library, University of North Carolina at Chapel Hill.

10. F. H. Johnston, "Excerpts from the Orange Presbytery," *North Carolina Presbyterian* (1883), Presbyterian Study Center, Montreat, North Carolina.

11. Obituary: John Chavis," *Watchman of the South* I, no. 47 (July 19, 1938), 191, Richmond VA.

12. Appiah, Kwame and Henry Louis Gates, eds. *Africana: The Encyclopedia of the African and African American Experience.* (New York: Basic Books, 1999), 413.

Epilogue

1. Civis Benet Puryear, "Against Public Schools for Negroes," *Southern Planter and Farmer,* December 1875, *Dabney Papers,* Duke University Perkins Library Archives.

2. *Ibid.*

3. Opal Winchester Hawkins, *From Brush Arbor to Bricks and Mortar: An Oral History of the Mount Zion Community of Greensboro, North Carolina* (Greensboro: 1984), 28.

II. Letter ... by the Reverend Dr. John Chavis

Introduction

1. F. H. Johnston, "Excerpts from the Orange Presbytery," *North*

Carolina Presbyterian (1883), Presbyterian Study Center, Montreat, North Carolina

2. Ernest Trice Thompson, *Presbyterians in the South, Vol. I: 1607–1861* (Richmond, VA: John Knox, 1963), 189.

3. Johnston.

4. *Ibid.*

5. Personal interview with the Rev. Mr. Phil Butin of the Oxford Presbyterian Church and the historic Nutbush Presbyterian Church, 1988.

6. Henry Pattillo, *Sermons*, August 3, 1787. Firestone Library Rare Book Room, Princeton University.

7. *Ibid.* These sermons were signed by Henry Pattillo, Granville County, North Carolina, June 14, 1878. It is to be noted that one of the subscribers in the list at the back of Pattillo's *Sermons* was Mr. Jacob Chavis. He is listed in the Mecklenburg County, Virginia Census for 1760–1790 and 1800. Choosing to reside on the Virginia side, he was probably a relative of Gibrea and William Chavis. He was also perhaps a member of Brim or Bluestone Church, located a few miles west of Clarksville. Mrs. Madrue Chavers-Wright wrote a letter to N. G. Hutchinson, Clerk of Circuit Court of Mecklenburg County, in Boydton, Virginia, commenting upon her research on John Chavis and his religious background. Mrs. Wright's letter was my first acquaintance with the connection between the churches and people of Mecklenburg County, Virginia, and the churches and people of Granville County, North Carolina.

8. John Chavis, *Letter Upon the Doctrine of the Extent of the Atonement of Christ* (Raleigh, NC: J. Gales and Son, 1837), 3, North Carolina Collection, University of North Carolina.

9. *Ibid.,* 3–4.

10. *Ibid.,* 4-5.

11. *Ibid.,* 8.

12. *Ibid.*

13. *Ibid.*

14. Compare Frank Kermode, "Institutional Control of Interpretation," *Salamagundi* 43 (Winter 1979), 72–83.

15. G.C. Shaw, *John Chavis* (Binghamton, NY: Vail-Ballou, 1931), 12.

16. Personal interview with Rev. George Crawfoot of the Grassy Creek Presbyterian Church in Stovall, Granville County, North Carolina, 1988.

17. Letter from G. W. Kittrell to Charles Phillips, May 18, 1883, *Charles Phillips Collection*, Southern Collection, University of North Carolina.

18. Chavis, 11, quotes Revelation 7:9.

Bibliography

Manuscript Collections

Cameron Collection, 1789–1860. Southern Historical Collection, Wilson Library, University of North Carolina at Chapel Hill.

Chavis, John. *Letter Upon the Doctrine of the Extent of the Atonement of Christ.* (Raleigh: J. Gales & Son, 1837). North Carolina Collection, Wilson Library, University of North Carolina at Chapel Hill.

____. Papers. Southern Historical Collection, Wilson, Library, University of North Carolina at Chapel Hill.

____. Sermon. North Carolina Collection, Wilson Library, University of North Carolina at Chapel Hill.

Downey, Samuel Smith, Papers. Perkins Library Manuscript Collection, Duke University.

Haywood, John, Papers. Southern Historical Collection, Wilson Library, University of North Carolina at Chapel Hill.

Horner, J.M. Letter to E. M. Oldham of New York. Southern Historical Collection, Wilson Library, University of North Carolina at Chapel Hill.

Knight, Edgar W. "Notes on John Chavis." *The North Carolina Historical Review* VII, no. 3 (July 1930), 336.

Madrue Chavers-Wright. Letter to N. G. Hutchinson, Clerk of Circuit Court, Mecklenburg County, Virginia, concerning John Chavis. Princeton University Archives, Princeton, New Jersey and Presbyterian Study Center, Montreat, North Carolina.

Mangum, Willie P., Collection. North Carolina Division of Archives and History, Raleigh.

____. Papers, 1825–1859. Library of Congress. Typescript in the Archives of the North Carolina Historical Commission, Raleigh. The papers have been edited by Henry Thomas Shanks (Raleigh: North Carolina Division of Archives and History, 1952).

Phillips, Charles, Collection. Southern Historical Collection, Wilson Library, University of North Carolina at Chapel Hill.

Pitman Papers. Bute County. North Carolina Division of Archives and History, Raleigh.

Willie, Rev. William, Estate Papers. North Carolina Division of Archives and History, Raleigh.

Other Primary Sources

Free Negroes and Slave Records. *Register of Free Negroes*. Nos. 1–2, 1809–1865. 1 reel. Virginia Archives.

Granville County, North Carolina. *Abstracts of Wills and Estate Records, 1746–1808*. Zoe Hargett Gwynn, ed. North Carolina Division of Archives and History, Raleigh.

_____. *Apprentice Bonds*. North Carolina Division of Archives and History, Raleigh.

_____. *Deeds, 1761*. North Carolina Division of Archives and History, Raleigh.

_____. *Grantees*. Book H. North Carolina Division of Archives and History, Raleigh.

_____. *Grantees 1746–1751*. Books A, B, C, E. North Carolina Division of Archives and History, Raleigh.

_____. *Index of Grantors, 1746–1869*. Books A, B, C, D, E, G, H, K, L, N, O, P, Q, R, T, V, and Z. Letter C in each book lists where Chavises granted land to settlers. Richard B. Thornton Library Genealogical Room, Oxford, North Carolina.

_____. *List of Taxables for 1762*. North Carolina Division of Archives and History, Raleigh.

_____. "List of Taxables for 1762 in Granville County and Census of Granville County." *North Carolina Genealogical Society Journal* XII, no. 3 (August 1986), 155.

_____. "Marriage Bonds." Elizabeth Hicks Hummell, ed. *Hicks' History of Granville County*, Vol. I (1965). Richard B. Thornton Library Genealogical Room, Oxford, North Carolina.

_____. *Marriages of Granville County, North Carolina, 1753–1868*. Brent H. Holcomb, comp. North Carolina Division of Archives and History, Raleigh.

_____. *North Carolina Census, 1784–1787*. Transcribed by Alvaretta Kenan Register. North Carolina Division of Archives and History, Raleigh.

_____. *United States Census, 1790–1910*. North Carolina Division of Archives and History, Raleigh.

Guardians' Accounts, 1788–93. Virginia Archives.

Guardians' Accounts, 1871–1873, 1876. Virginia Archives.

Guardians' Bonds, 1765–1831. Virginia Archives.

Guardians' Books, 1800–1835. Virginia Archives.

Halifax County, North Carolina. *Inventory of Estate Records.* "A True and Perfect Inventory of all the goods and chattels... of James Milner, Esq., deceased." North Carolina Division of Archives and History, Raleigh.

_____. *Inventory of the Estate of James Milner, 1775.* North Carolina Division of Archives and History, Raleigh.

Indenture. W. P. Mangum to James Webb and Thomas D. Watts, April 25, 1828. The Willie P. Mangum Collection. North Carolina Division of Archives and History, Raleigh.

Inventories ... Accounts of Sale, 1783–1904, Virginia Archives.

"John Chavis School," Advertisement in the *Raleigh Register*, Thursday, August 26, 1808.

Marriage Bonds and Consents, 1770–1850. Virginia Archives

Mebane, C. H. "Report on John Chavis from Superintendent of Public Instruction of North Carolina from 1896–1898." Presbyterian Study Center, Montreat, North Carolina.

Mecklenburg County, Virginia. *Census of Free Blacks, 1790 ff.* Virginia Archives.

_____. *Deeds, 1765–1893.* Virginia Archives.

_____. *First Census of the United States, 1790.* Virginia Archives.

_____. *Indentures, 1794–1837.* Virginia Archives.

_____. *Index to Old Orders of Interest, 1793.* Virginia Archives.

_____. *List of Slaves, 1863–1864.* Virginia Archives.

_____. *List of Slaves, 1790 ff.* Virginia Archives.

_____. *Marriage Bonds and Consents, 1770–1850.* Virginia Archives.

_____. *Marriages, Returns of Ministers, 1785–1854.* 2 vols. and Index. Virginia Archives.

_____. *Mecklenburg County 1780–1798, 1790–1810.* (12 volumes). Virginia Archives.

_____. *Quarterly Court Records, 1796–1802,* 1 vol. Virginia Archives.

_____. *Records of State Enumerations, 1782–1785.* Virginia Archives.

_____. *Revolutionary War Pensions and Bounty Land-Warrant Application Files.* Washington, D.C., 1974. National Archives.

_____. *Virginia 1830 Census Index.* Virginia Archives.

_____. *Wills, 1764–1967.* Virginia Archives.

Minutes of the Lexington Presbytery. October 19, 1799. Vol. III, 158. Presbyterian Study Center, Montreat, North Carolina.

_____. October 23, 1800–October 25, 1800. Presbyterian Study Center, Montreat, North Carolina.

_____. November 18–19, 1800. Presbyterian Study Center, Montreat, North Carolina.

_____. June 9, 1801. Presbyterian Study Center, Montreat, North Carolina.

North Carolina Estate Records. Granville County. Gibrea Chavis to William Chavis. July 1777. North Carolina Division of Archives and History, Raleigh.

Pension Records, Service Records, Revolutionary War. Adjutants General's
    Office, Old Records Division, National Archives, Washington. An *Index
    of the Revolutionary Records in the Virginia Archives* was compiled
    by Dr. H.J. Eckenrode in 1912 and 1914. John H.G. Wathney published
    Historical Register of Virginians in the Revolution 1775–1783, intro-
    duction by H.J. Eckenrode (Richmond VA: Dietz, 1938). These docu-
    ments contain records of John Chavis service in the Revolutionary War.
Presbyterian Church. *Minutes of the General Assembly.* Presbyterian His-
    torical Society (1799–1838), Philadelphia.
Presbyterian General Assembly. *Excerpts from Minutes of the Study Com-
    mittee of Missions of the Presbyterian Church....* Presbyterian Histor-
    ical Society, Philadelphia, Pennsylvania.
Princeton University. *Minutes of the Trustees, 1788–1796.* Seeley G. Mudd
    Library, Princeton University Archives.
_____. *Minutes of the Trustees, 1790–1810.* On microfilm.
Rockbridge County, Virginia. *County Court Record, 1802.* Virginia Archives.
_____. *Rockbridge County Court Order Book, #6, 10.* Rockbridge County
    Court House Records.
Ruffner, W. H. "Notes on Chavis." Written in long hand. The Historical
    Foundation of the Presbyterian and Reformed Churches, Montreat,
    North Carolina.
Surry County, Virginia. *Wills, Estate Accounts and Inventories, 1730–1800*
    by Lyndon H. Hart, III. Virginia Archives.
Wake County, North Carolina. *Affidavit.* Edgar H. Goold in reference to
    Sarah Walker and Collins Walker; Hannah Jones and Ernest Jones.
    Mortgage to Saint Augustine's College. 13th February, 1930. *Wake
    County Register of Deeds.*
_____. Deed. Andrew Syme to Sarah Walker. August 29, 1873. *Wake County
    Register of Deeds*, 184–186.
_____. Deed. Gatsey Mitchell and Alfred Mitchell to William Chavis, heirs.
    July 5, 1870. *Wake County Register of Deeds*, 529–531.
_____. Deed. Gatsey Mitchell to John Chavis, Lizzie Austin, and Sally
    Chavis. August 20, 1870. *Wake County Register of Deeds.*
_____. Deed. John Chavis to William E. Roberts and William Holloway.
    1822. *Wake County Register of Deeds.*
_____. Deed. Sarah Walker and Collins Walker; Hannah Jones and Ernest
    Jones. Mortgage on their property from A. B. Hunter, Treasurer of
    Saint Augustine's Normal School. June 15, 1914. *Wake County Regis-
    ter of Deeds*, 348–349.
_____. Deed. To Sarah Walker, Louisa Ray, and Isabelle Mitchell. August
    21, 1873. *Wake County Register of Deeds.*
_____. *North Carolina Census and Tax Abstracts: 1830 and 1840.* Frances
    Holloway Wynne, comp. North Carolina Division of Archives and His-
    tory, Raleigh.

_____. *Real Estate Conveyances, 1800–1805.* North Carolina Division of Archives and History, Raleigh.

_____. *Real Estate Conveyances, 1806–1807.* North Carolina Division of Archives and History, Raleigh.

_____. *Real Estate Conveyances, 1811 and 1813.* North Carolina Division of Archives and History, Raleigh.

_____. *Real Estate Conveyances, 1815.* North Carolina Division of Archives and History, Raleigh.

_____. *United States Census, 1800–1910.* North Carolina Division of Archives and History, Raleigh.

Will Books, County Court Order Books, List of Taxables, Guardian Books, Marriage Bonds, for the following counties:

 Chatham County, North Carolina (Pittsboro).
 Granville County, North Carolina (Oxford).
 Halifax County, North Carolina (Halifax).
 Orange County, North Carolina (Hillsboro).
 Wake County, North Carolina (Raleigh).
 Brunswick County, Virginia (Lawrenceville).
 Lunenberg County, Virginia (Sussex).
 Sussex County, Virginia (Sussex).
 Mecklenburg County, Virginia (Boydton).

Books and Monographs

Ashe, Samuel A'Court. *History of North Carolina.* 2 vols. Raleigh: Edwards and Broughton, 1925.

Babcock, Theodore S. *Manumission in Virginia 1782–1806.* M.A. thesis, University of Virginia, August 1974.

Barber, Jesse B. *A History of the Work of the Presbyterian Church Among the Negroes in the United States of America.* New York: Board of National Missions of the Presbyterian Church in the U.S.A., 1936.

Ballagh, James Curtis. *A History of Slavery in Virginia.* Baltimore: Johns Hopkins University Press, 1902.

Bassett, John Spencer. *Slavery and Servitude in the Colony in North Carolina.* Baltimore: Johns Hopkins University Press, 1896.

Battle, Kemp Plummer. *History of the University of North Carolina.* 2 vols. Raleigh: Edwards and Broughton, 1907, 1912.

Berlin, Ira. *Slaves Without Masters.* New York: Pantheon, 1974.

Boyd, Daniel L. *Free-Born Negro: The Life of John Chavis.* B.A. thesis, Princeton University, 1947.

Boyd, William K. *History of North Carolina.* Chicago: Lewis, 1919.

Brawley, Benjamin G. *Negro Builders and Heroes.* Chapel Hill: University of North Carolina Press, 1937.

Bruce, Phillip Alexander. *The Plantation Negro as a Freeman*. New York: Putnam, 1889.

Brumbaugh, Gaius Marcus. *Revolutionary War Records*. Lancaster PA: Lancaster Press, 1936.

Butterfield, Roger. *The American Past*. New York: Simon and Schuster, 1947.

Chavis, John. *Letter Upon the Doctrine of the Extent of the Atonement of Christ*. Raleigh NC: J. Gales and Son, 1837.

Collins, V. L. *President Witherspoon: A Biography*. Princeton NJ: The Princeton University Press, 1928.

Connor, R.D.W. *North Carolina*. New York: American Historical Association, 1929.

Coon, Charles L. *North Carolina Schools and Academies 1790–1840, A Documentary History*. Raleigh: Edwards and Broughton, 1915.

Corbitt, David. *The Formation of North Carolina Counties*. Raleigh: North Carolina Archives.

Craven, Avery O. "Poor Whites and Negroes in the Ante-bellum South." *Journal of Negro History* XV (January 1930), 14–25.

Davis, Robert P. *Virginia Presbyterians in American Life: Hanover Presbytery (1755–1980)*. Richmond VA: Hanover Presbytery, 1982.

Foote, W. H. *Sketches of North Carolina*. New York: R. Carter, 1846.

Franklin, John Hope. *The Free Negro in North Carolina*. Chapel Hill: The University of North Carolina Press, 1943.

_____. *From Slavery to Freedom: A History of American Negroes*. New York: Alfred A. Knopf, 1947.

Green, Ashbel. *Presbyterian Missions*. New York: Anson, D. F. Randolph & Co., 1893.

Gwathney, John H. *Historical Register of Virginians in the Revolution*. Richmond VA: Dietz, 1928.

Heinegg, Paul. *Free African Americans of North Carolina and Virginia*. Baltimore: Genealogical, 1994.

Hill, Michael. "Historical Research Report: The Mangum Family Cemetery, Durham, North Carolina." January 4, 1984. North Carolina Archives.

Hinshawe, William W., et. al., eds. *Encyclopedia of American Quakers' Genealogy*. Ann Arbor, MI: 1942.

Hockett, Henry Carey. *Political and Social Growth of the American People*. New York: Macmillan, 1942.

Holcomb, Brent Howard, ed. and comp. *Bute County, North Carolina, Minutes of the Court of Pleas and Quarter Sessions, 1767–1779*. Raleigh: State Library of North Carolina, 1988.

Jackson, Luther P. *Free Negro Labor and Property Holding in Virginia*. New York: D. Appleton Century, 1942.

James, Marquis. *Andrew Jackson: Portrait of a President*. New York: Bobbs-Merrill, 1937.

Johnson, Guion Griffin. *Ante-bellum North Carolina*. Chapel Hill: University of North Carolina Press, 1937.

Jordan, Winthrop. *White Over Black*. Chapel Hill: University of North Carolina Press, 1968.

Kaplan, Sidney. *The Black Presence in the Era of the American Revolution, 1770–1800*. Washington DC: National Portrait Gallery, Smithsonian Institution, 1973.

Knight, Edgar W. *The Academy Movement in the South*. N.p., n.d.

Konkle, Burton and Alva. *John Motley Moorehead and the Development of North Carolina*. Philadelphia: William J. Campbell, 1922.

Lefler, Hugh Talmage, and Albert Ray Newsome. *North Carolina: The History of a Southern State*. Chapel Hill: University of North Carolina Press, 1954.

McClelland, Thomas C. *Historical Address to the Rhode Island Home Missionary Society*. Newport RI: Milne, 1900.

McColley, Robert. *Slavery in Jeffersonian Virginia*. Champaign: University of Illinois Press, 1964.

Morrison, William B. *The Red Man's Trail*. Richmond VA: Presbyterian Committee of Publication, 1932.

Murray, Andrew E. *Presbyterians and the Negro—A History*. Philadelphia: Presbyterian Historical Society, 1966.

Murray, Elizabeth Reid. *Wake: Capital County of North Carolina*. Vol. I. Raleigh: Capital County, 1983.

Pattillo, Henry. *Sermons*. August 3, 1787. Firestone Library Rare Book Room, Princeton University.

_____. *A Geographical Catechism*. Chapel Hill: University of North Carolina Press, 1900.

Peace, Samuel T. *"Zeb's Black Baby": Vance County, North Carolina, A Short History*. Henderson NC: 1955.

Perdue, Theda. *Slavery and the Evolution of Cherokee Society: 1540–1866*. Knoxville: University of Tennessee Press, 1979.

The Princeton Book. Boston: Houghton, Osgood and Company; Cambridge Riverside: 1879.

Quarles, Benjamin. *The Negro in the American Revolution*. Chapel Hill: University of North Carolina Press, 1961.

Quick, W. H. *Negro Stars in All Ages of the World*. Richmond: S.B. Adkins, 1898.

Raper, Charles Lee. *The Church and Private Schools in North Carolina: A Historical Study*. Greensboro NC.

Ray, Worth S. *Colonial Granville County and Its People*. *"Loose Leaves from the Lost Tribes of North Carolina."* Baltimore: Genealogical, 1965.

Russell, John H. *The Free Negro in Virginia, 1619–1865*. Baltimore: Johns Hopkins University Press, 1913.

Schlesinger, Arthur M., Jr. *The Age of Jackson.* Boston: Little, Brown, 1946.

Seawell, Joseph Lacey. *Low Tales for Laymen and Wayside Tales from North Carolina.* Raleigh NC: Edwards and Broughton, 1929.

Shanks, Henry T. *Papers of Willie P. Mangum.* Vol. II, 1833–1838. Raleigh: North Carolina Archives and History, 1952.

Shaw, G. C. *John Chavis.* Binghamton NY: Vail-Ballou, 1931.

Siler, David W., comp. *The Eastern Cherokees: A Census of the Cherokee Nation in North Carolina, Tennessee, Alabama, and Georgia in 1851.* Cottonport, Louisiana: Polyanthos, 1972.

Smith, Charles Lee. *The History of Education in North Carolina.* Washington DC: Government Printing Office, 1888.

Smith, Elwyn Allen. *The Presbyterian Ministry in American Culture.* Philadelphia: Westminster.

Smith, John Blair. *Address Delivered Before the Northern Missionary Society in the State of New York.* Schenectady NY: Wyckoff, 1797.

Stone, Robert H. *A History of Orange Presbytery, 1770–1790.* Greensboro NC: 1970.

Swain, David L. *Early Times in Raleigh.* R. S. Tucker, Comp. Raleigh NC: Walker, Hughes, 1867.

Synott, Marcia G. *The Half-Opened Door: Researching Admission Discrimination at Harvard, Yale and Princeton.* Chicago: University of Chicago Press, 1982.

Thompson, Ernest Trice. *Presbyterians in the South, Vol I: 1607–1861.* Richmond VA: John Knox, 1963.

Toole, Christine Townes. *The Life and Times of John Chavis.* Unpublished thesis. North Carolina Central University, Durham NC, 1956.

Washington, Booker T. *The Story of the Negro.* New York: Doubleday, Page, 1909.

Wathoney, John H. *Historical Register of Virginians in the Revolution: 1775–1783.* Introduction by H. J. Eckenrode. Virginia Archives.

Wheeler, John H. *Historical Sketches of North Carolina to 1850.* Philadelphia: Lippincott, Grombo, 1850.

White, William S. *The African Preacher.* Philadelphia: Presbyterian Editor of Education, 1849.

Woodson, Carter G. *The Education of the Negro Prior to 1861.* 2nd ed. Washington DC: Association for the Study of Negro Life and History, 1919.

_____. *Free Negro Heads of Families in the United States in 1830.* North Carolina Archives.

_____. *Negro Makers of History.* 5th ed. Washington DC: Associated Publishers, 1968.

Articles

Bassett, John Spencer. *Suffrage in the State of North Carolina.* Annual report of the American Historical Association, 1895. Pp. 269–385.

Blacknall, C. W. "Negro Slave Holders and Slave Owners." *The [Raleigh] News and Observer* (Thursday, October 31, 1895). The John Spencer Bassett Papers. Perkins Library Archives, Duke University.

Capehart, L.B. "Naming the Negro Park." *The [Raleigh] News and Observer* (September 13, 1937), 4.

"Census of Granville County." *North Carolina Genealogical Society Journal* XII, no. 3, 155.

Connor, R. W. *Address Delivered Before the Unveiling and Presentation of the Bust of William Gaston by the North Carolina Bar Association.* Raleigh: Edwards & Broughton, 1914.

"Crowd at Chavis Park Dedication." *The [Raleigh] News and Observer* (May 11, 1938), 16.

Delany, L. T. "Blount Park." *The [Raleigh] News and Observer* (September 6, 1937), 4.

Des Champs, Margaret Burr. "John Chavis As a Preacher to Whites." *North Carolina Historical Review* 32 (1955).

Devane, Carl. "Work Has Just Begun." *News and Observer* (September 9, 1937), 4.

Gregory, W. H. "History of Old Shiloh Presbyterian Church. "*Presbyterian Standard* (April 11, 1906 and April 25, 1906), passim.

Hudson, Gossie H. "John Chavis, 1763–1838: A Social-Psychological Study." *The Journal of Negro History* LXIV, no. 2 (Spring 1979), 142–156.

Jackson, Luther P. "Manumission in Certain Virginia Cities." *Journal of Negro History* XV (July 1930).

_____. "Virginia Negro Soldiers and Seamen in the American Revolution." *The Journal of Negro History* XXIII, no. 3 (July 1942), 247–287.

_____. "Religious Instruction of Negroes, 1830–1860." *Journal of Negro History* XV, 72 ff.

Jernigan, Marcus W. "Slavery and Conversion in the American Colonies." *American Historical Review* 21, 504–527.

"John Chavers." *The Raleigh Sentinel* and reprinted in *The Oxford Torchlight*, September 21, 1880. Article was found by Barbara Parramore. See *Dictionary of North Carolina Biography*, Vol. I, 358.

"John Chavis." *The North Carolina Presbyterian* XVII, no. 337 (January 23, 1884).

"John Chavis." *Negro Year Book, 1918–1919.* Pp. 235–236.

Johnston, F. H. "Excerpts from the Orange Presbytery." *North Carolina Presbyterian* (1883).

Kermode, Frank. "Institutional Control of Interpretation." *Salmagundi* 43 (Winter 1979), 72–83.

Knight, Edgar W. "Notes on John Chavis." *The North Carolina Historical Review* VII, no. 3 (July 1930).

Lee, John W. "Brief Sketch of the Presbyterian Church in the United States: The Negroes, Especially During the Last Sixty Years." N.p., n.d.

"Negroes Enjoy Holiday in New Recreational Park." *The [Raleigh] News and Observer* (July 6, 1937), 10.

Nicol, M. B. "Naming a Park." *The [Raleigh] News and Observer* (Sept. 21, 1937), 4.

"Obituary: John Chavis." *Watchman of the South* [Richmond VA] I, no. 47 (July 19, 1838), 191.

"Open Negro Park Today." *The [Raleigh] News and Observer* (June 22, 1937), 5.

Parramore, Barbara. "John Chavis." *Dictionary of North Carolina Biography*, Vol. I (1979), 358.

Randall, Annie G. "John Chavis." *(North Carolina) State Normal Magazine* X (1905).

"Revolutionary War Service Records and Settlements." *North Carolina Genealogical Society Journal* VIII, no. 4 (November 1982), 209.

Savage, W. S. "The Influence of John Chavis and Lunsford Lane." *Journal of Negro History* XXV, 14–24.

Seawell, Joseph Lacy. "Black Teacher of Southern Whites." *The New York Times Magazine* (May 18, 1924), 8.

_____. "Strange Forgotten Days of the Old South." *The [Raleigh] News and Observer* (March 23, 1930), 7.

_____. "John Chavis, a Remarkable Negro." [Raleigh] *News and Observer* (March 13, 1930), 48.

Smith, C. L. "WPA Recreation Park to Honor John Chavis." *The [Raleigh] News and Observer* (May 8, 1938), 20.

"Virginia Negro Soldiers and Seamen in the American Revolution." *The Journal of Negro History* XXVII, no. 3 (July 1942), 247 ff.

Walker, [name unknown]. "John Chavis." *The North Carolina Presbyterian* XVII, no. 337 (January 31, 1883).

"Washington and Lee University: A National Historic Landmark." Richmond: Virginia State Library, 1973.

Weeks, Stephen B. "John Chavis, Ante-bellum Negro." *The Southern Workman* (February 1914).

"Worth Remembering," *The [Raleigh] News and Observer* (Sept. 15, 1937), 4.

Zebinsky, William. "The Population Geography of the Free Negro in Ante-bellum America." *Population Studies* III, no. 4 (March 1950).

Interviews

Mrs. Inez Brooks of Raleigh, North Carolina. 1988.

Reverend Phil and Reverend Jan Butin, ministers of the Oxford Presbyterian Church, Granville County, North Carolina, and the historic Nutbush Presbyterian Church, Vance County, North Carolina. 1988.

Reverend Geroge Crawfoot, minister of the historic Grassy Creek Presby-
    terian Church, Stovall, North Carolina, 1988.
Mrs. Mildred Harris of Bahama, North Carolina (Durham County), 1987.
Mrs. Asa Turner of Raleigh, North Carolina, 1988.

Newspapers and Periodicals

The Assembly's Missionary Magazine of Evangelical Intelligencer. Philadel-
    phia, 1805–1835.
Files of *The Raleigh Register,* 1790–1838.
Files of *The Star,* Raleigh NC, 1809–1839.
Watchman of the South, Richmond VA, 1801–1838.
Religious Remembrance, Philadelphia, 1811–1833.
Panoplist and Missionary Herald, Philadelphia, 1820.
The Oxford [NC] Searchlight or *Torchlight,* September 28, 1880.
The Hillsboro Recorder, Hillsboro[ugh] NC.

Index